Translation & Adaptation,
Retouch, Lettering and Design -
Kitty Media

© ASIA WATANABE 2003
Originally published in Japan in 2003 by HOUBUNSHA, Tokyo.
English translation rights arranged with HOUBUNSHA, Tokyo,
through TOHAN CORPORATION, Tokyo. Kitty Media office of
publication 519 8th Avenue, 14th floor, New York, NY 10018.

Kitty Press
Office of publication 519 8th Avenue, 14th floor
New York, NY 10018.

ISBN: 1-59883-021-X

Printed in Canada.

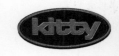

Because I'm a Boy!

BECAUSE I'M A BOY...3

SHAPE OF LOVE...21

ROPES OF LOVE...53

LION ON FRIDAY...63

SHEEP AND BANDAGE...89

RAIN OF LOVE...115

SHOW ME...133

CANDY AND WHIP...159

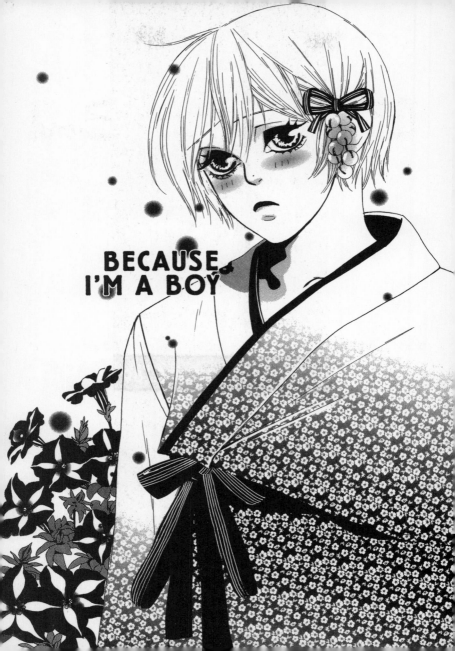

BECAUSE
I'M A BOY

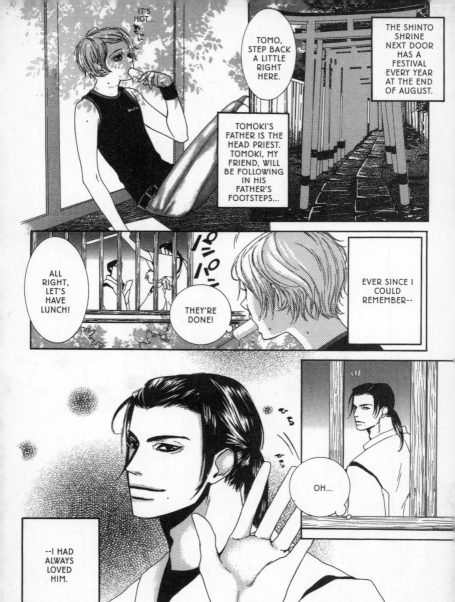

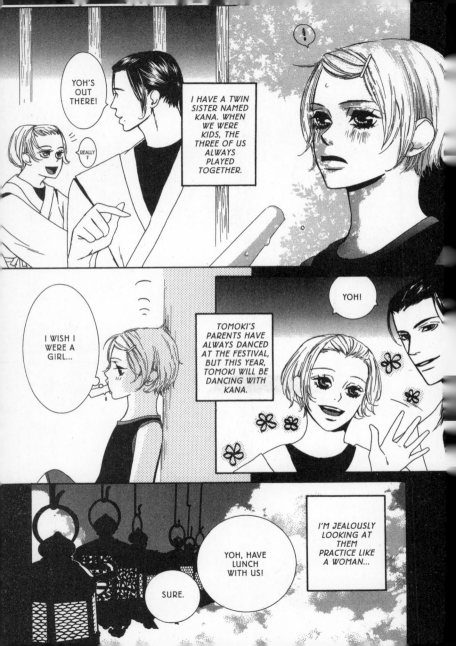

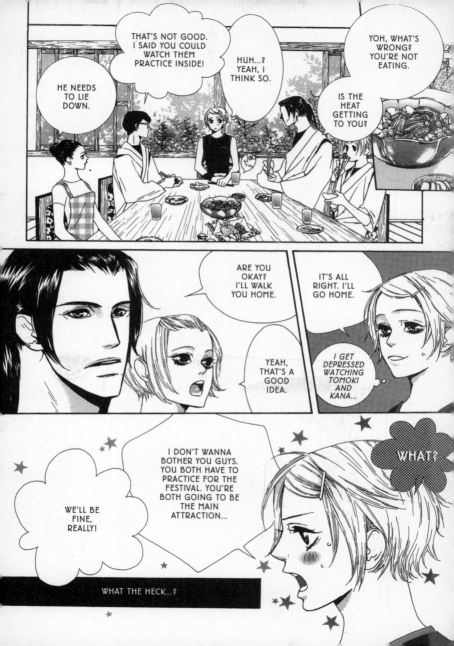

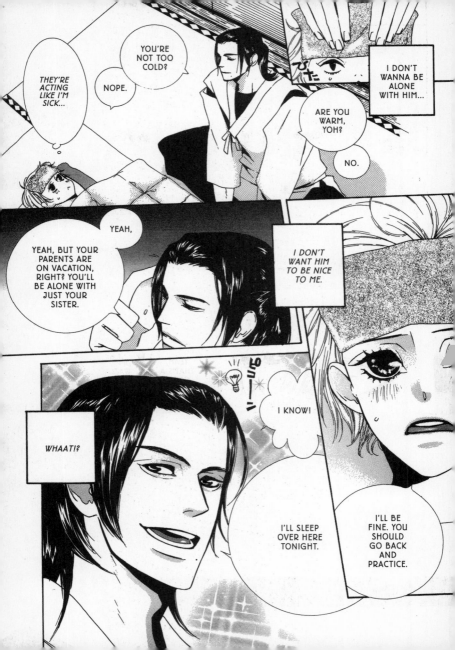

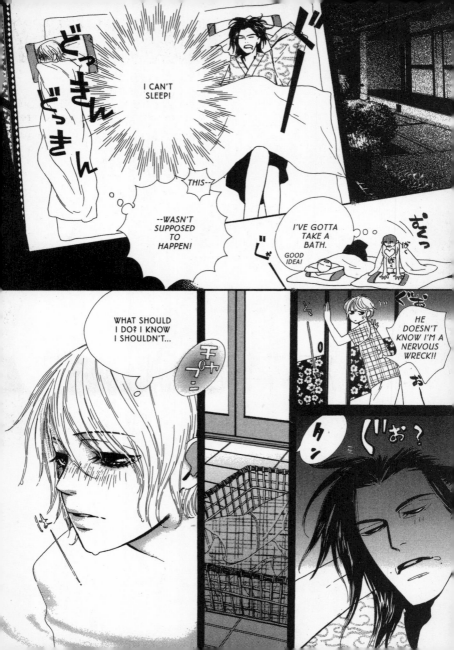

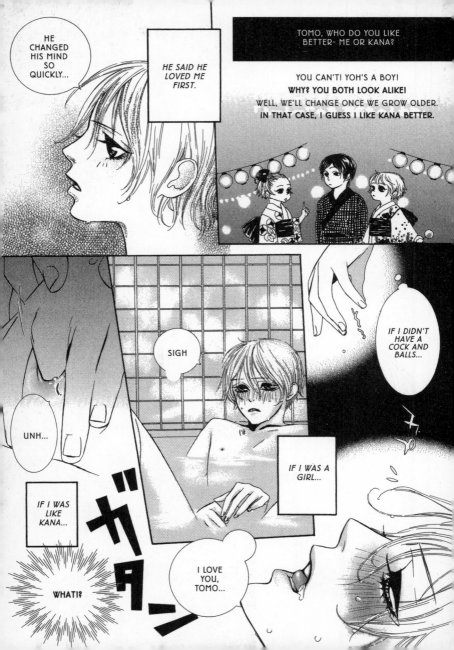

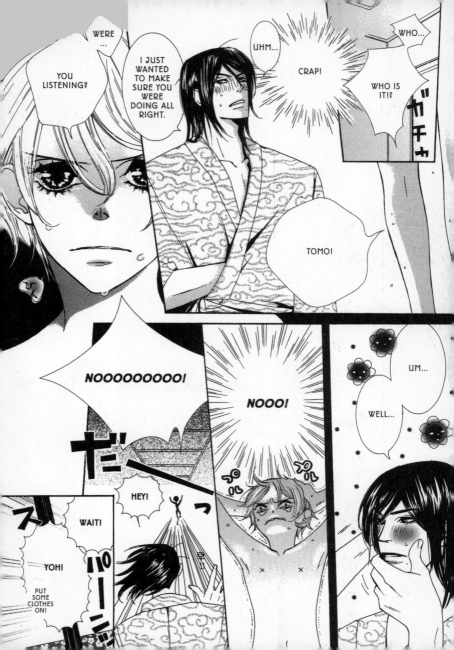

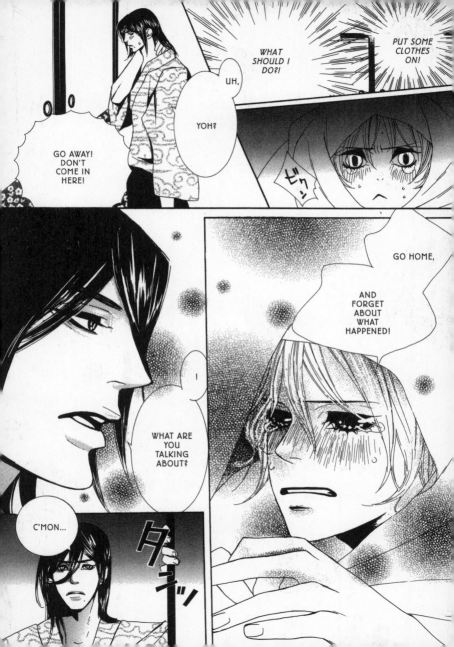

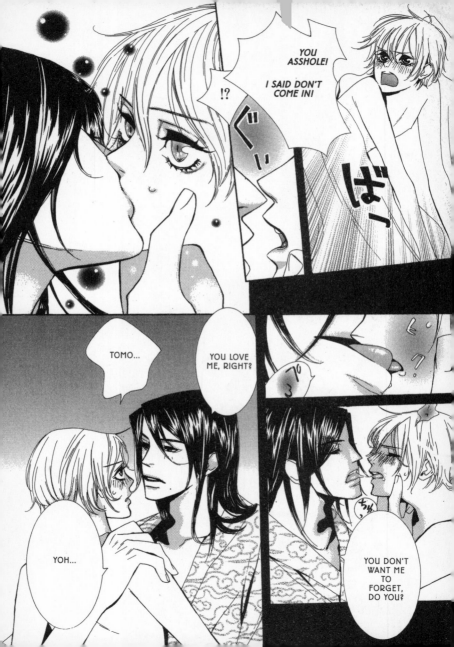

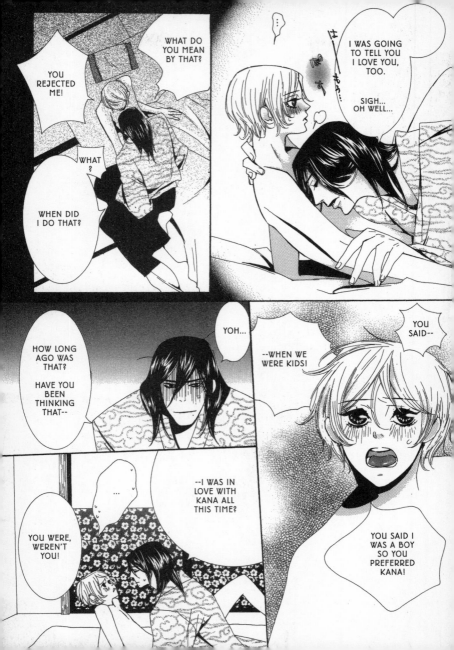

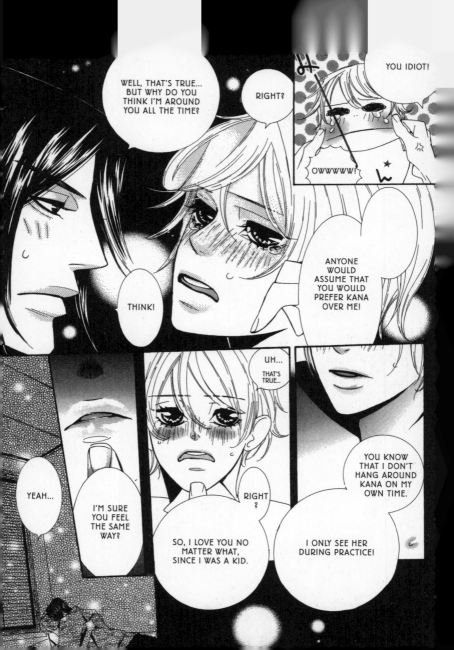

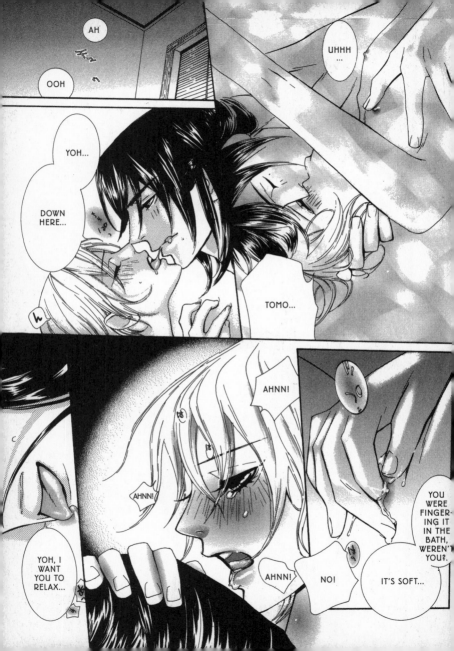

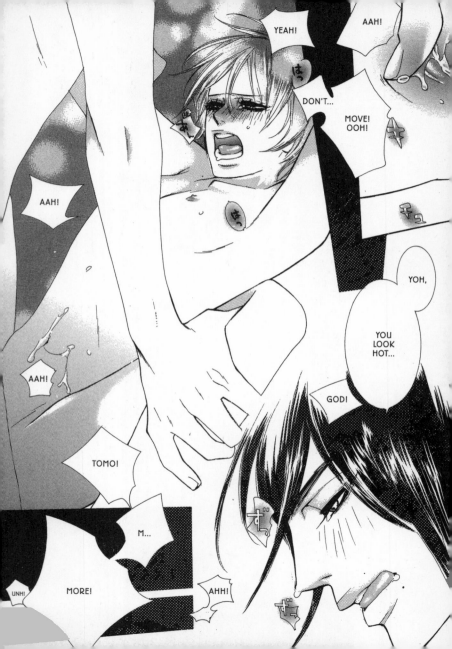

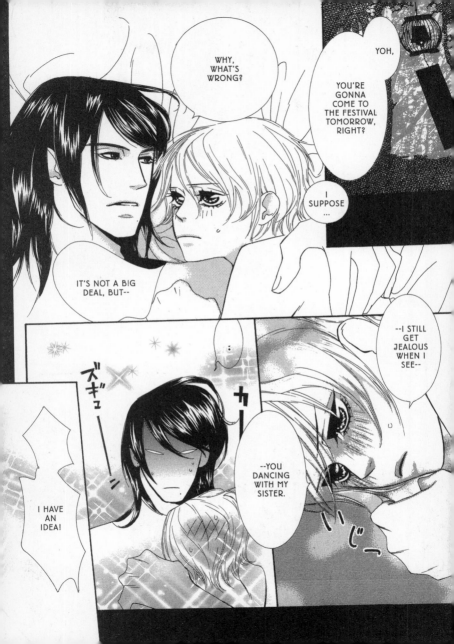

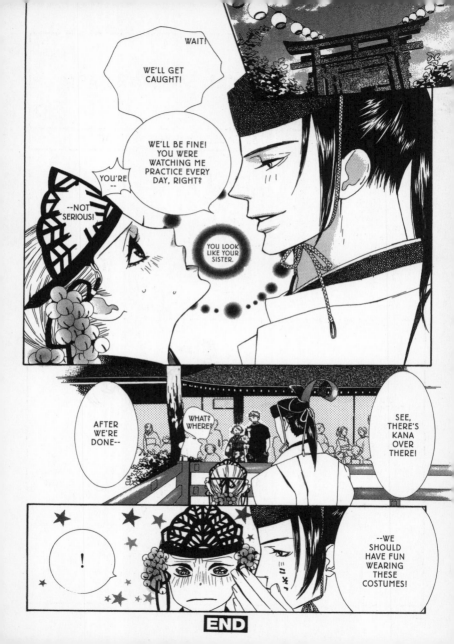

END

TROPICAL ECCENTRIC ASIA

BECAUSE I'M A BOY EPISODE

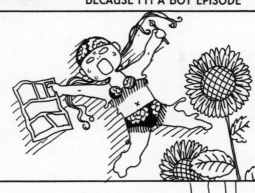

MY APARTMENT WAS SO STUFFY AND HOT! I WAS DYING FROM THE HEAT. ONE DAY, WHILE I WAS SHAVING MY UNDERARMS...

IT WAS SUMMER-TIME WHEN I WAS WORKING ON "BECAUSE I'M A BOY."

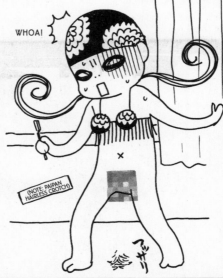

I DID DISCOVER THAT NOT HAVING HAIR HELPS KEEP ME COOL... (I PLAN ON DOING THIS EVERY YEAR NOW). *I TOLD MY EDITOR, AND SHE THOUGHT I WAS JOKING. IT'S THE TRUTH... AND NOW, MY NEW NICKNAME IS HAIRLESS CROTCH. (HA HA)

I HAD REALIZED I HAD SHAVED EVERY-WHERE.

Because I'm a Boy!

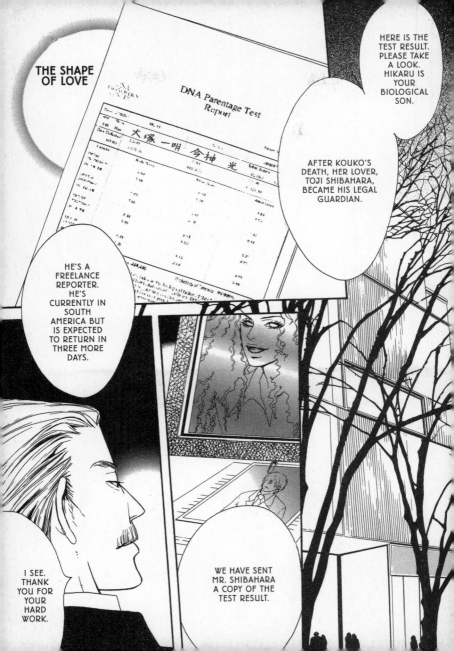

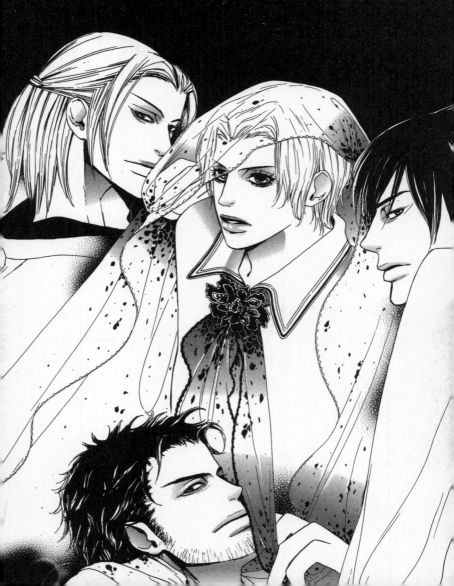

THE SHAPE
OF LOVE

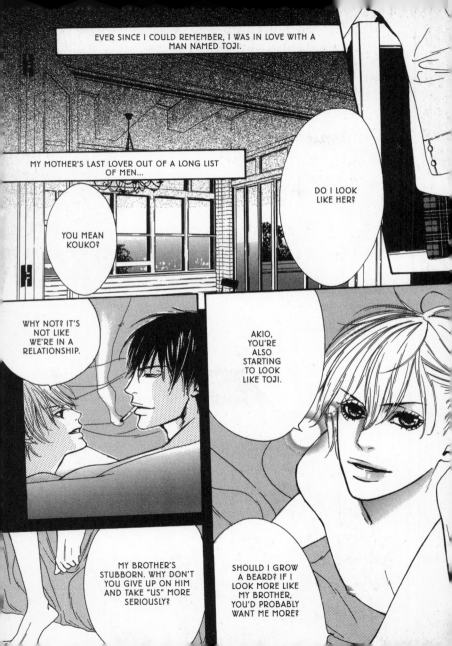

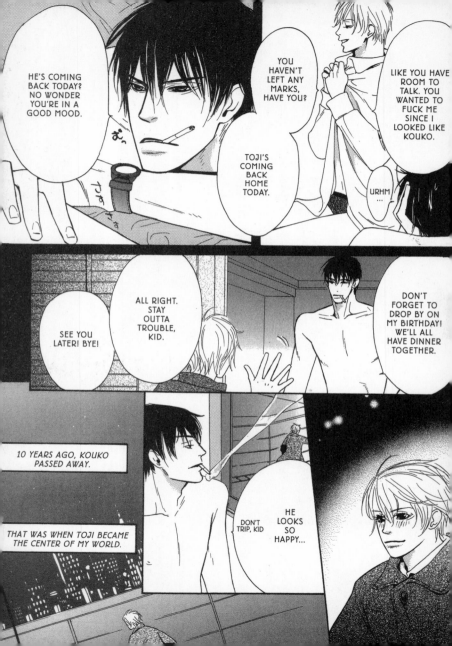

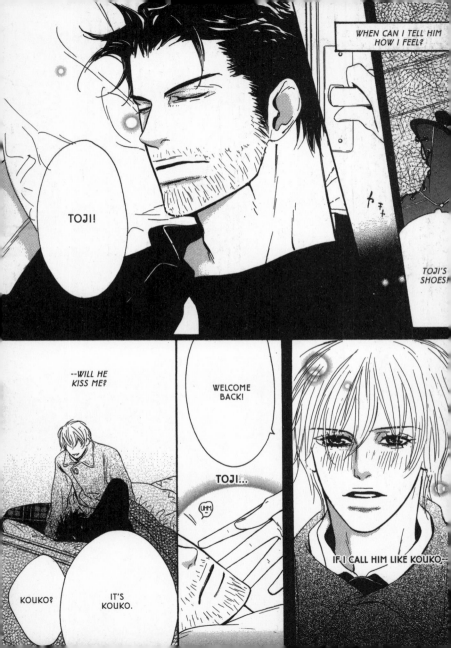

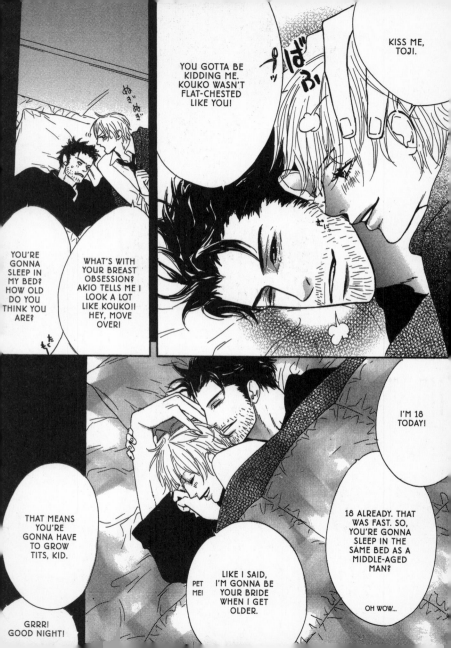

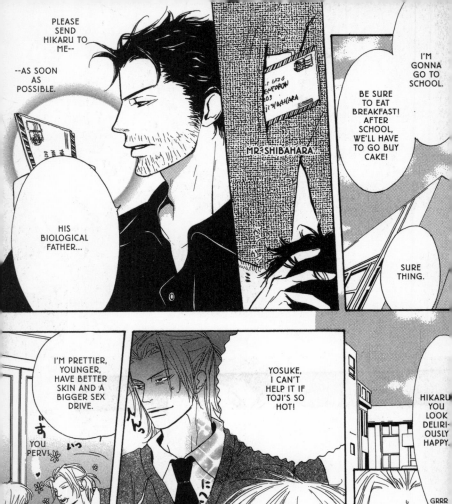

PLEASE SEND HIKARU TO ME--

--AS SOON AS POSSIBLE.

HIS BIOLOGICAL FATHER...

MR. SHIBAHARA

I'M GONNA GO TO SCHOOL.

BE SURE TO EAT BREAKFAST! AFTER SCHOOL, WE'LL HAVE TO GO BUY CAKE!

SURE THING.

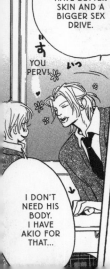

I'M PRETTIER, YOUNGER, HAVE BETTER SKIN AND A BIGGER SEX DRIVE.

YOU PERV!

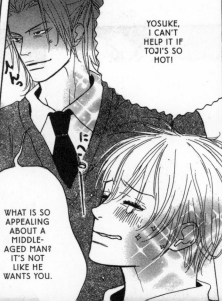

YOSUKE, I CAN'T HELP IT IF TOJI'S SO HOT!

WHAT IS SO APPEALING ABOUT A MIDDLE-AGED MAN? IT'S NOT LIKE HE WANTS YOU.

I DON'T NEED HIS BODY. I HAVE AKIO FOR THAT...

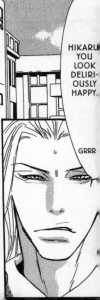

HIKARU YOU LOOK DELIRI-OUSLY HAPPY.

GRRR

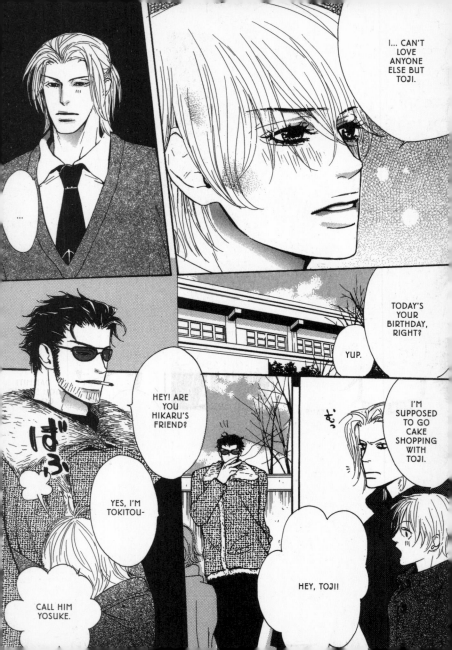

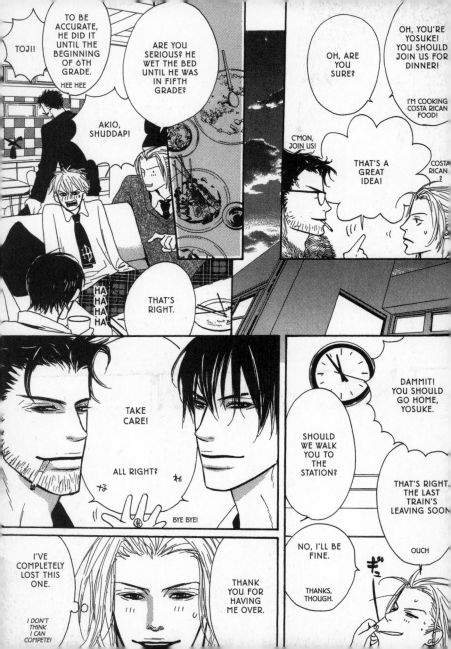

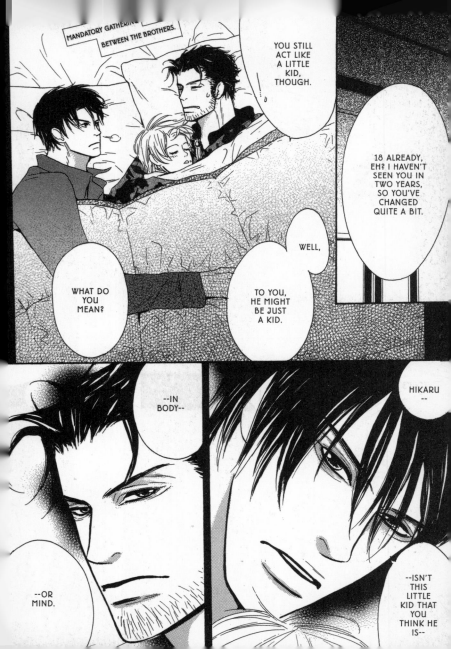

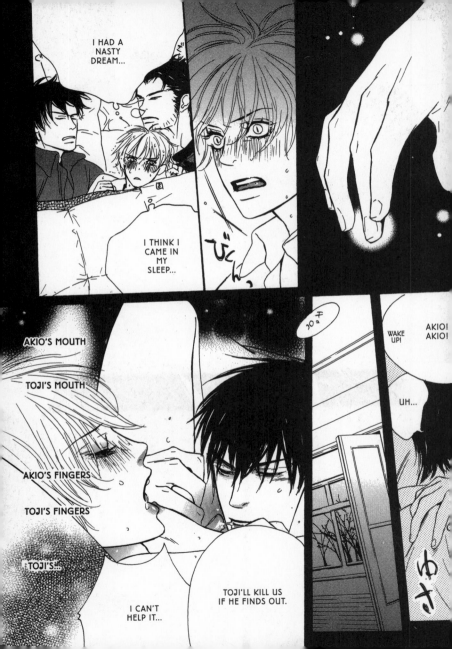

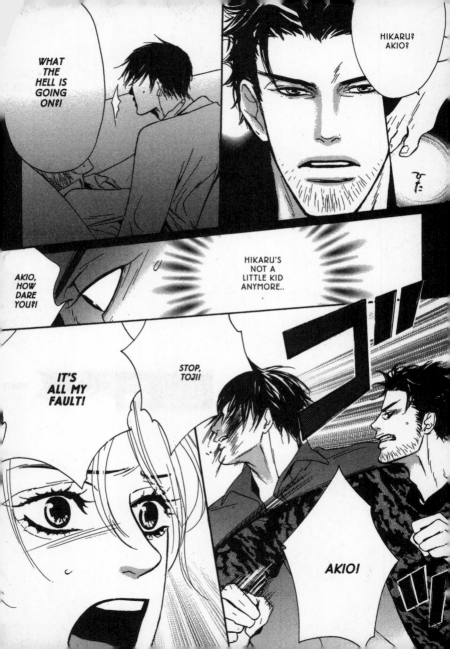

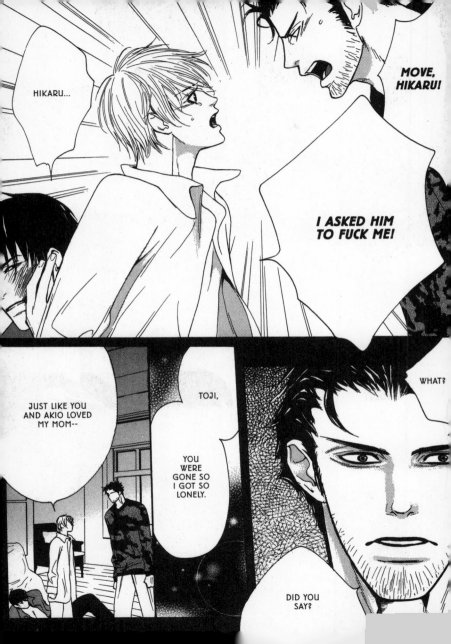

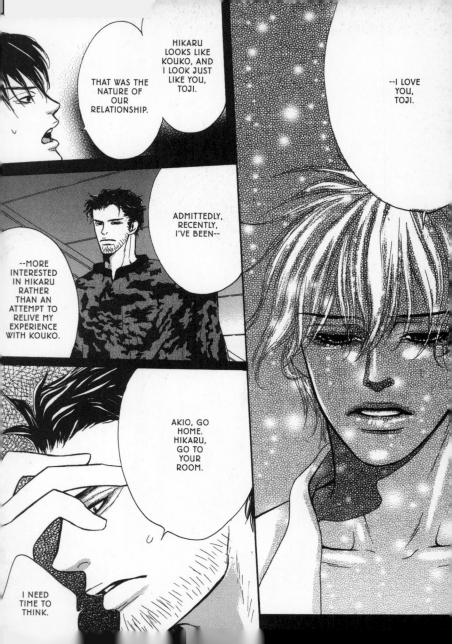

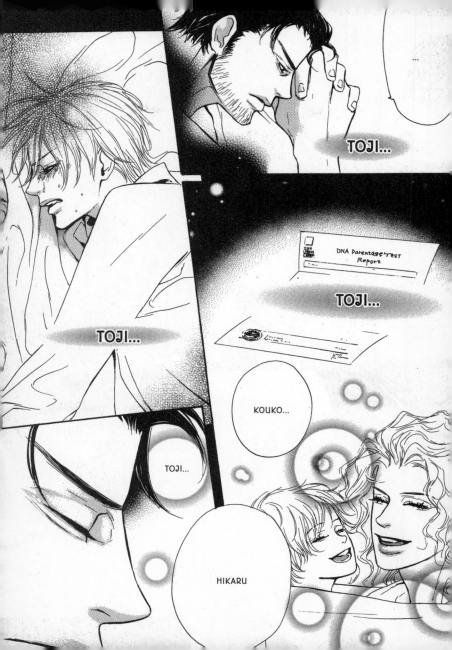

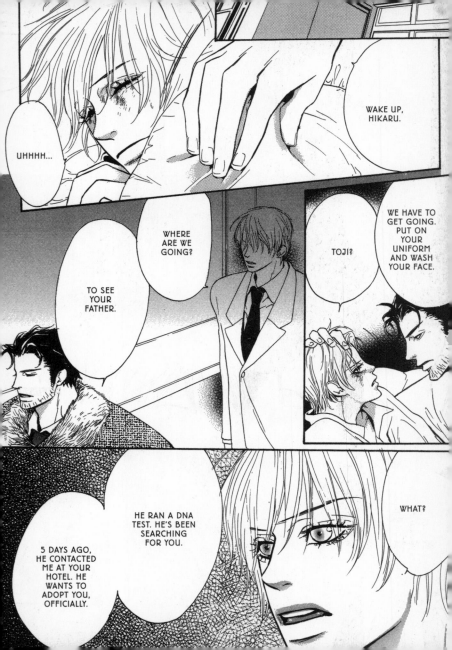

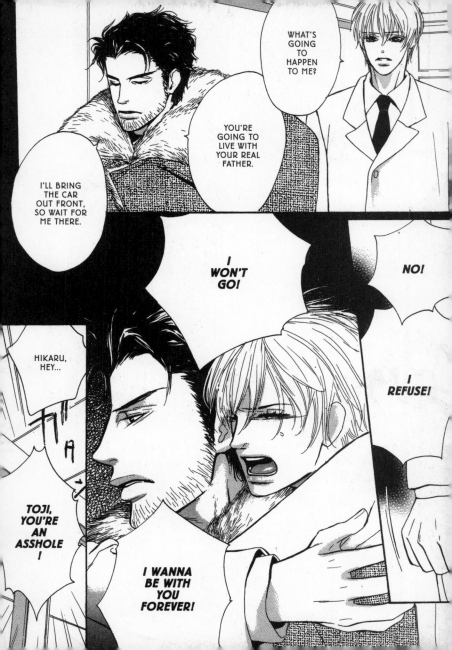

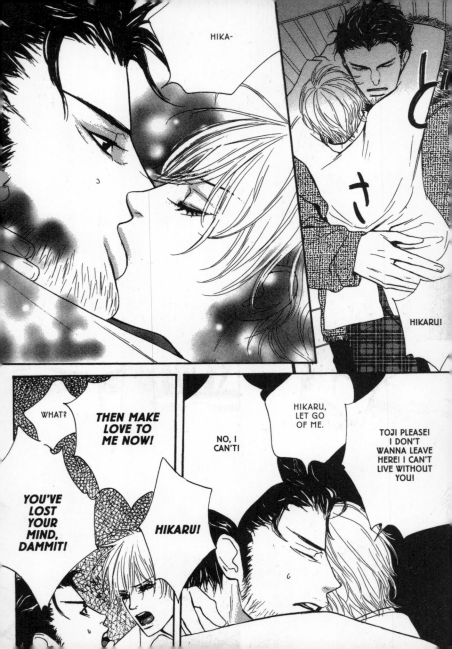

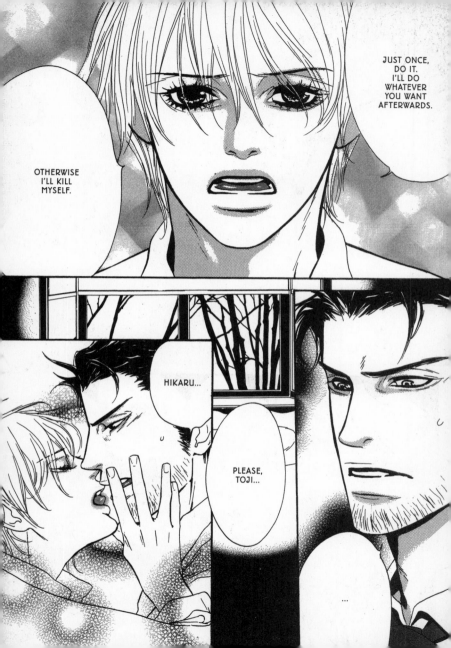

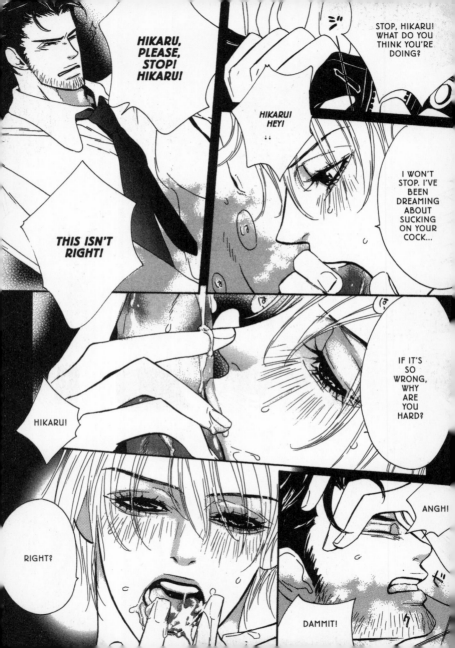

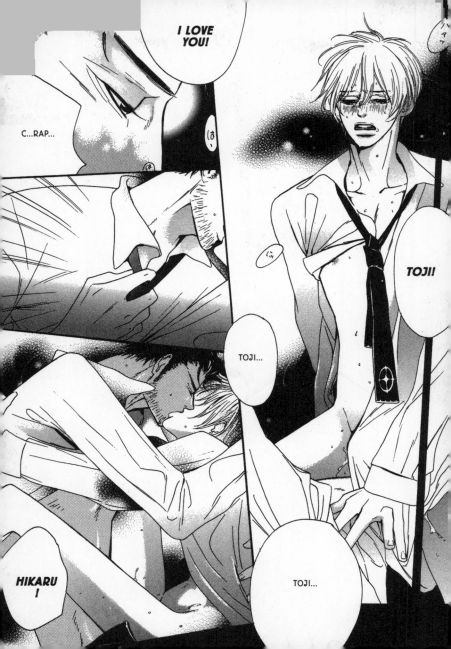

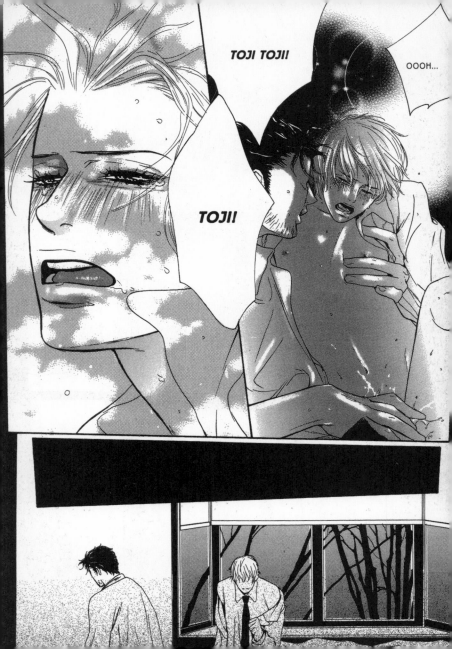

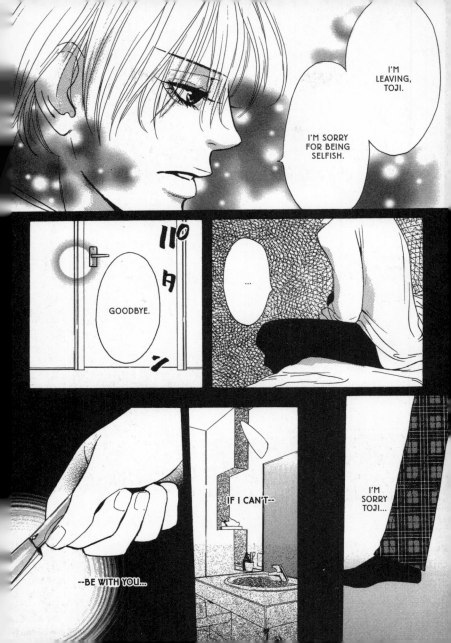

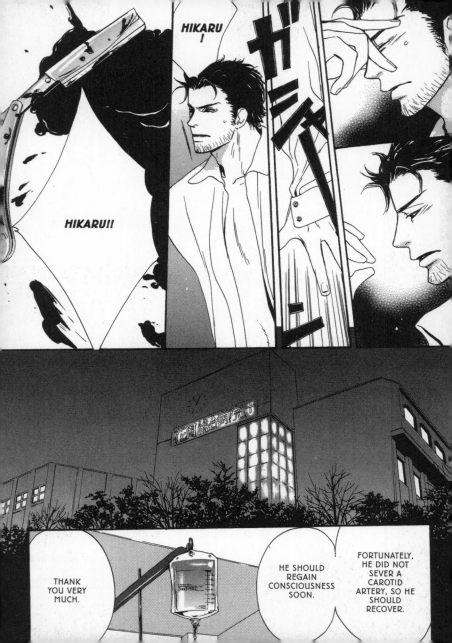

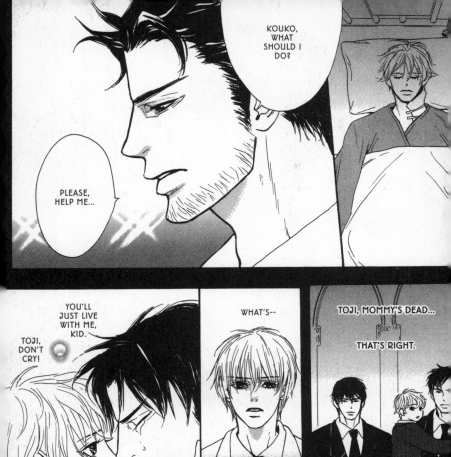

KOUKO, WHAT SHOULD I DO?

PLEASE, HELP ME...

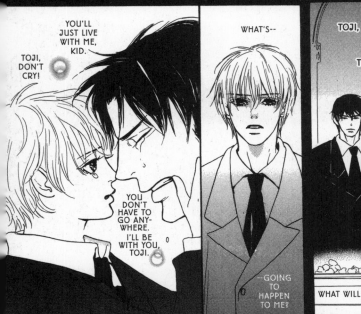

YOU'LL JUST LIVE WITH ME, KID.

TOJI, DON'T CRY!

YOU DON'T HAVE TO GO ANY- WHERE.

I'LL BE WITH YOU, TOJI.

WHAT'S--

--GOING TO HAPPEN TO ME?

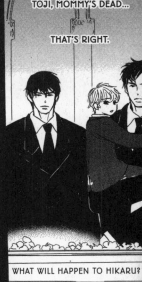

TOJI, MOMMY'S DEAD...

THAT'S RIGHT.

WHAT WILL HAPPEN TO HIKARU?

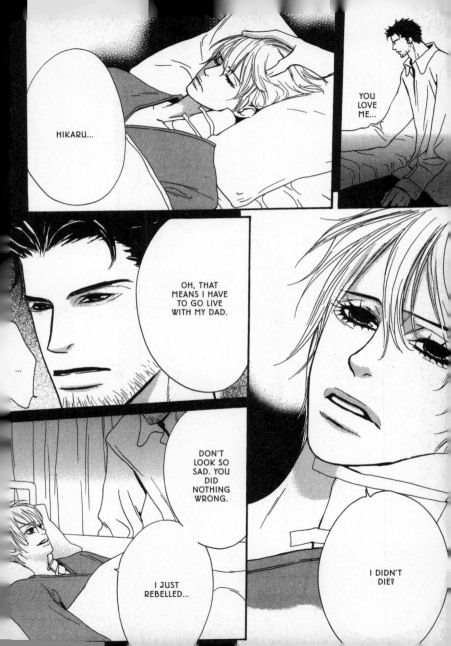

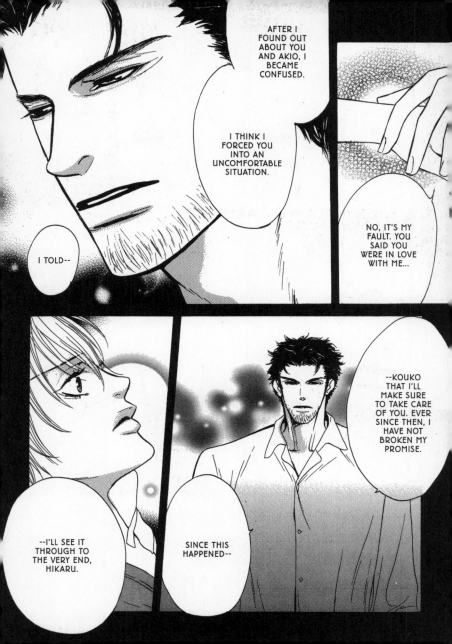

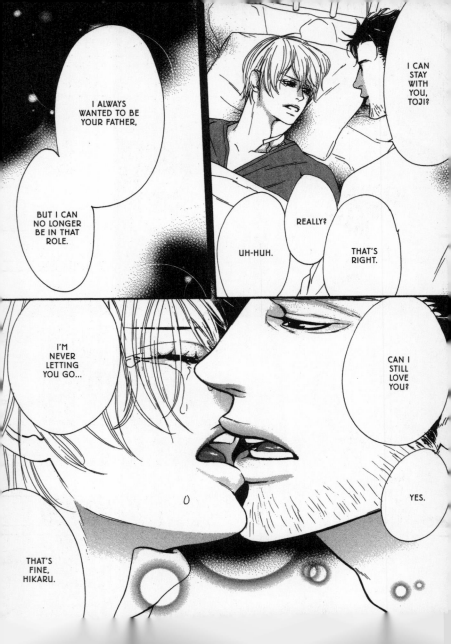

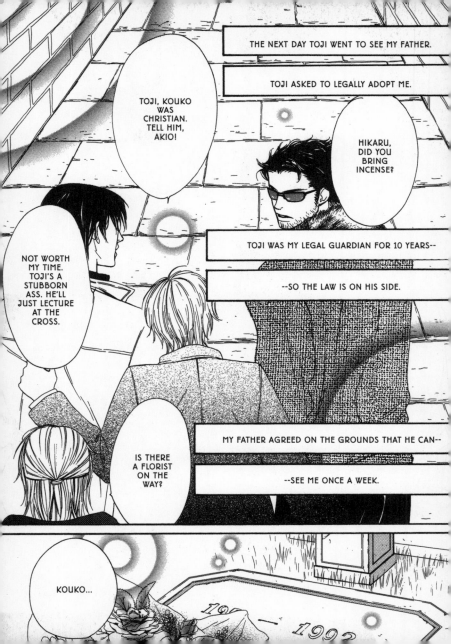

THE NEXT DAY TOJI WENT TO SEE MY FATHER.

TOJI ASKED TO LEGALLY ADOPT ME.

TOJI, KOUKO WAS CHRISTIAN. TELL HIM, AKIO!

HIKARU, DID YOU BRING INCENSE?

NOT WORTH MY TIME. TOJI'S A STUBBORN ASS. HE'LL JUST LECTURE AT THE CROSS.

TOJI WAS MY LEGAL GUARDIAN FOR 10 YEARS--

--SO THE LAW IS ON HIS SIDE.

IS THERE A FLORIST ON THE WAY?

MY FATHER AGREED ON THE GROUNDS THAT HE CAN--

--SEE ME ONCE A WEEK.

KOUKO...

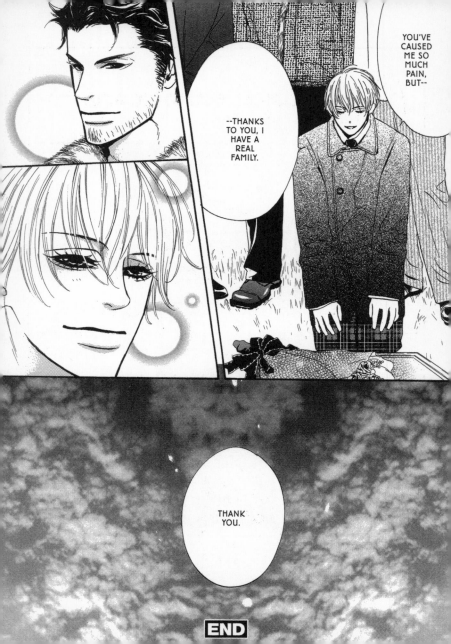

TROPICAL ECCENTRIC ASIA

SHAPE OF LOVE EPISODE

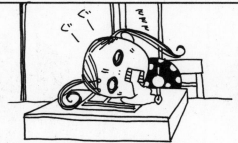

THERE WAS A HIGH SCHOOL NEAR MY APARTMENT.

WHEN I WAS WORKING ON THIS, IT WAS FALL.

*I WOULD REPEATEDLY DROOL ON MY ARTWORK, AND THEN I'D HAVE TO START OVER...

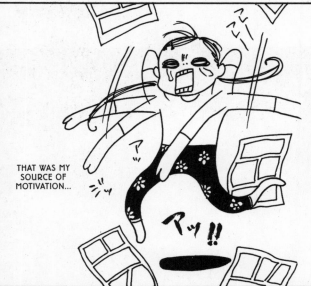

JUST GET TO WORK ...

THAT WAS MY SOURCE OF MOTIVATION...

I RECKLESSLY DECIDED TO TURN 30 PAGES OF ROUGH DRAFT INTO FINISHED PIECES. I WAS DUMB. IN THE MIDDLE, I WOULD CHEER WITH THE BRASS BAND PLAYING DURING A GAME.

Because I'm a Boy!

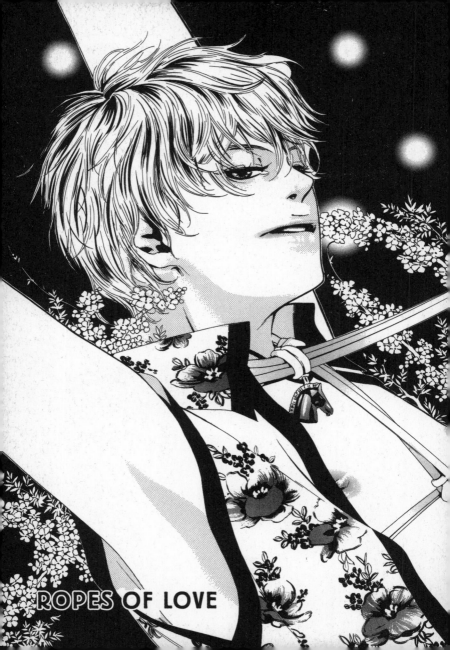

ROPES OF LOVE

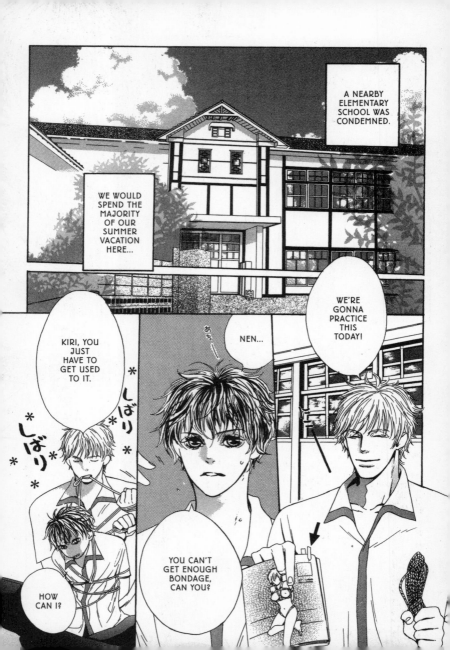

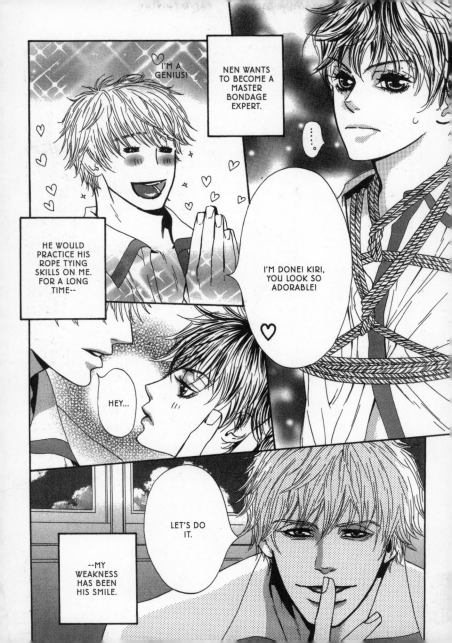

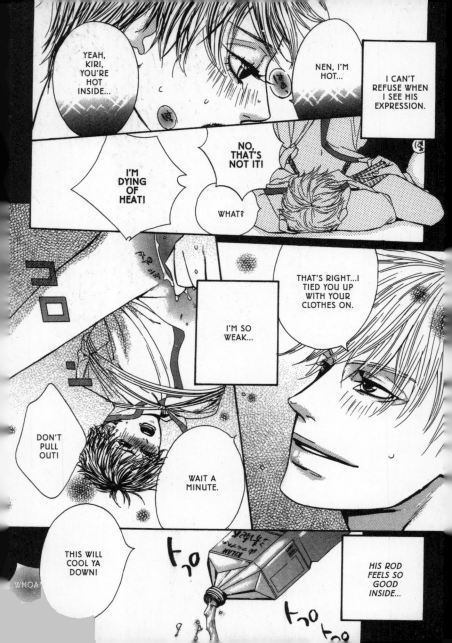

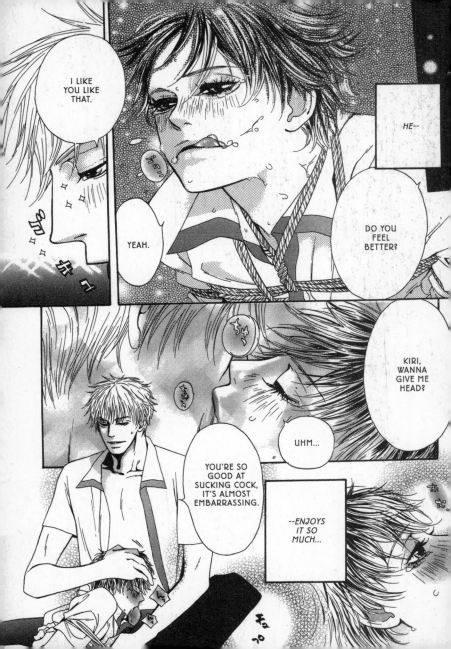

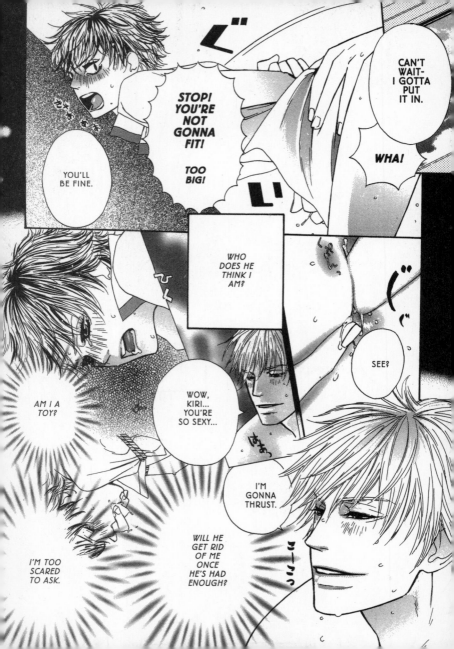

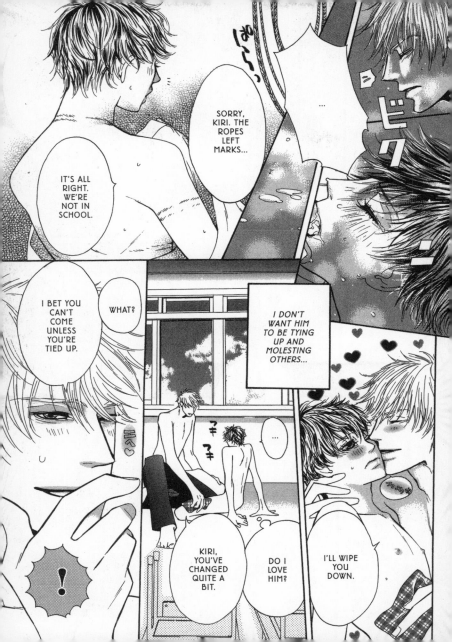

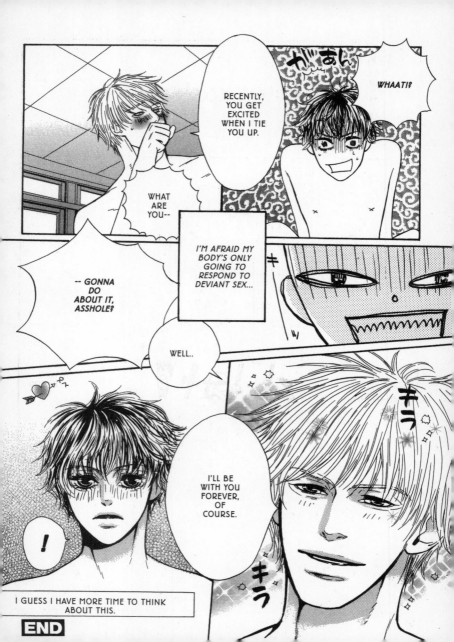

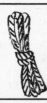

TROPICAL ECCENTRIC ASIA

ROPES OF LOVE EPISODE

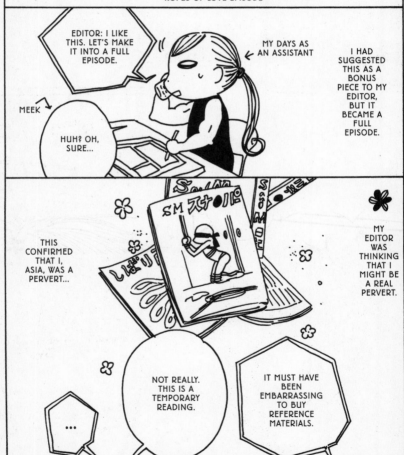

EDITOR: I LIKE THIS. LET'S MAKE IT INTO A FULL EPISODE.

MY DAYS AS AN ASSISTANT

I HAD SUGGESTED THIS AS A BONUS PIECE TO MY EDITOR, BUT IT BECAME A FULL EPISODE.

MEEK

HUH? OH, SURE...

THIS CONFIRMED THAT I, ASIA, WAS A PERVERT...

MY EDITOR WAS THINKING THAT I MIGHT BE A REAL PERVERT.

NOT REALLY. THIS IS A TEMPORARY READING.

IT MUST HAVE BEEN EMBARRASSING TO BUY REFERENCE MATERIALS.

...

Because I'm a Boy!

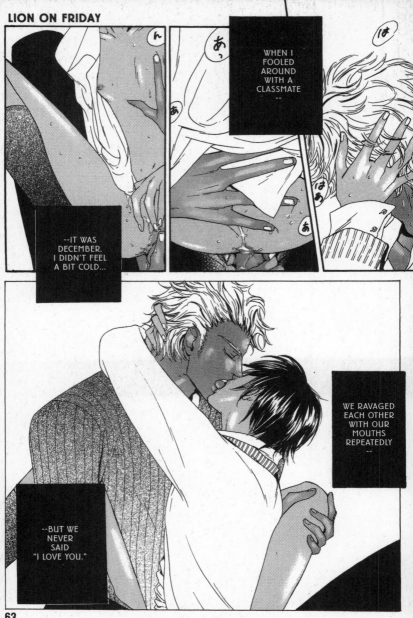

WHEN I FOOLED AROUND WITH A CLASSMATE --

--IT WAS DECEMBER. I DIDN'T FEEL A BIT COLD...

WE RAVAGED EACH OTHER WITH OUR MOUTHS REPEATEDLY --

--BUT WE NEVER SAID "I LOVE YOU."

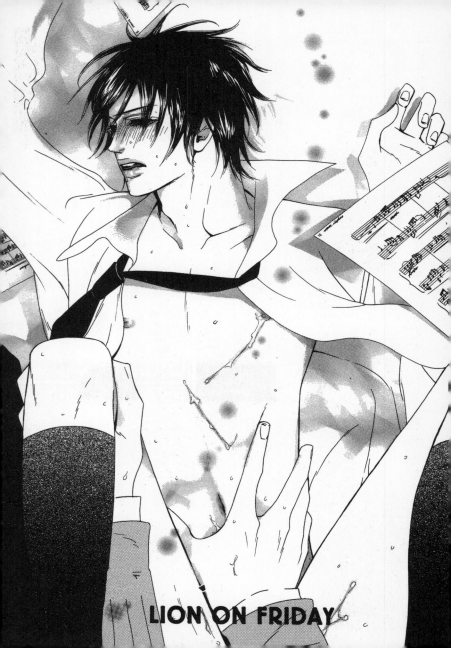

LION ON FRIDAY

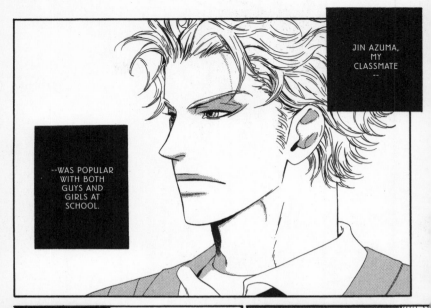

JIN AZUMA,
MY
CLASSMATE
--

--WAS POPULAR
WITH BOTH
GUYS AND
GIRLS AT
SCHOOL.

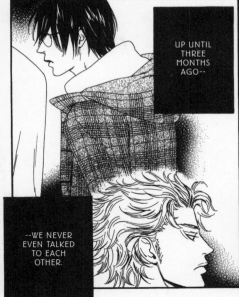

UP UNTIL
THREE
MONTHS
AGO--

--WE NEVER
EVEN TALKED
TO EACH
OTHER.

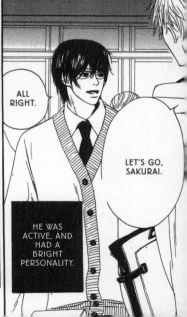

ALL
RIGHT.

LET'S GO,
SAKURAI.

HE WAS
ACTIVE, AND
HAD A
BRIGHT
PERSONALITY.

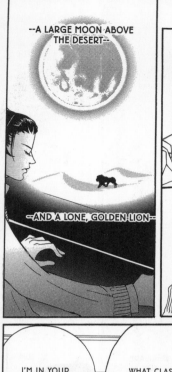

--A LARGE MOON ABOVE THE DESERT--

--AND A LONE, GOLDEN LION--

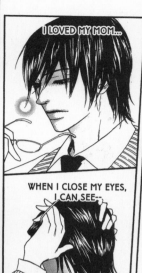

I LOVED MY MOM...

WHEN I CLOSE MY EYES, I CAN SEE--

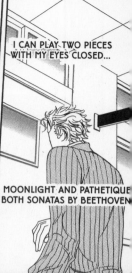

I CAN PLAY TWO PIECES WITH MY EYES CLOSED...

MOONLIGHT AND PATHETIQUE BOTH SONATAS BY BEETHOVEN

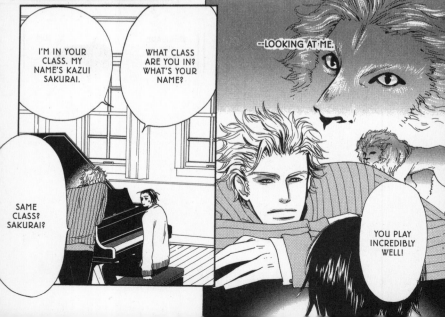

I'M IN YOUR CLASS. MY NAME'S KAZUI SAKURAI.

WHAT CLASS ARE YOU IN? WHAT'S YOUR NAME?

SAME CLASS? SAKURAI?

--LOOKING AT ME.

YOU PLAY INCREDIBLY WELL!

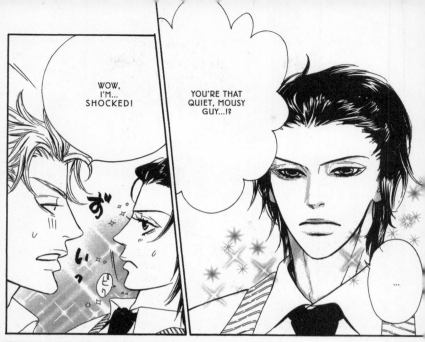

WOW, I'M... SHOCKED!

YOU'RE THAT QUIET, MOUSY GUY...!?

...

THIS IS RIGHT ABOVE THE TRACK. ARE YOU ALWAYS HERE AFTER SCHOOL?

NO, JUST ON FRIDAYS, SINCE THE BRASS BAND PRACTICES DURING THE REST OF THE WEEK.

I SEE...

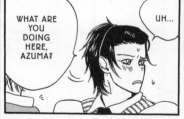

WHAT ARE YOU DOING HERE, AZUMA?

UH...

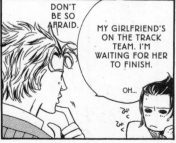

DON'T BE SO AFRAID.

MY GIRLFRIEND'S ON THE TRACK TEAM. I'M WAITING FOR HER TO FINISH.

OH...

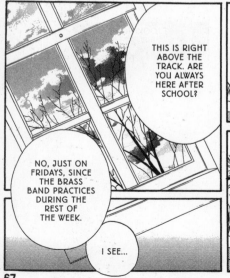

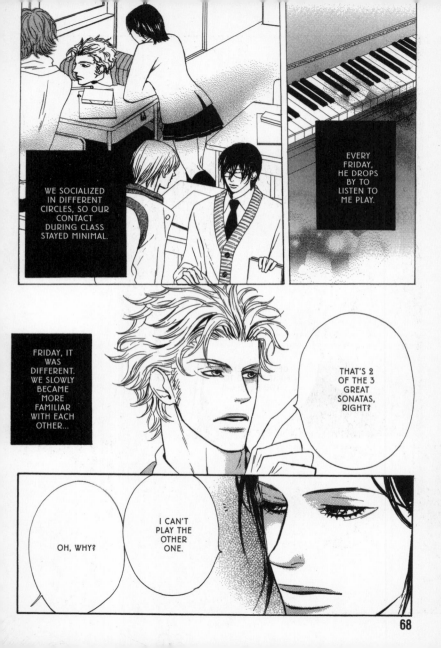

WE SOCIALIZED IN DIFFERENT CIRCLES, SO OUR CONTACT DURING CLASS STAYED MINIMAL.

EVERY FRIDAY, HE DROPS BY TO LISTEN TO ME PLAY.

FRIDAY, IT WAS DIFFERENT. WE SLOWLY BECAME MORE FAMILIAR WITH EACH OTHER...

THAT'S 2 OF THE 3 GREAT SONATAS, RIGHT?

I CAN'T PLAY THE OTHER ONE.

OH, WHY?

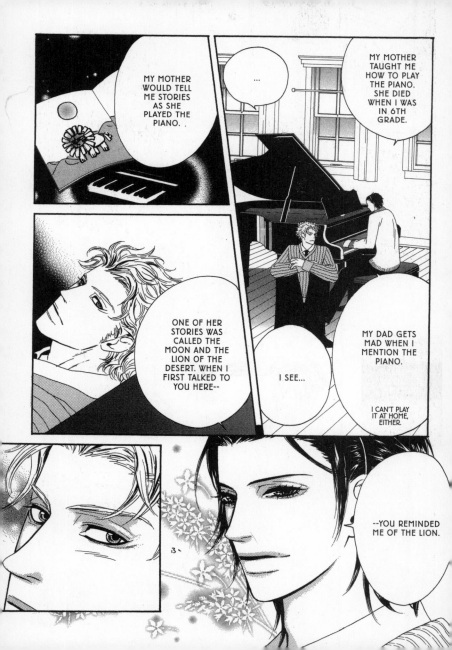

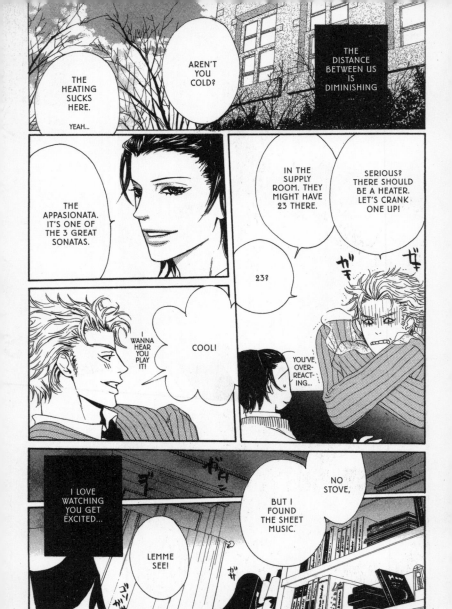

THE HEATING SUCKS HERE.

YEAH...

AREN'T YOU COLD?

THE DISTANCE BETWEEN US IS DIMINISHING...

THE APPASIONATA. IT'S ONE OF THE 3 GREAT SONATAS.

IN THE SUPPLY ROOM. THEY MIGHT HAVE 23 THERE.

SERIOUS? THERE SHOULD BE A HEATER. LET'S CRANK ONE UP!

23?

I WANNA HEAR YOU PLAY IT!

COOL!

YOU'VE OVER-REACT-ING...

I LOVE WATCHING YOU GET EXCITED...

NO STOVE,

BUT I FOUND THE SHEET MUSIC.

LEMME SEE!

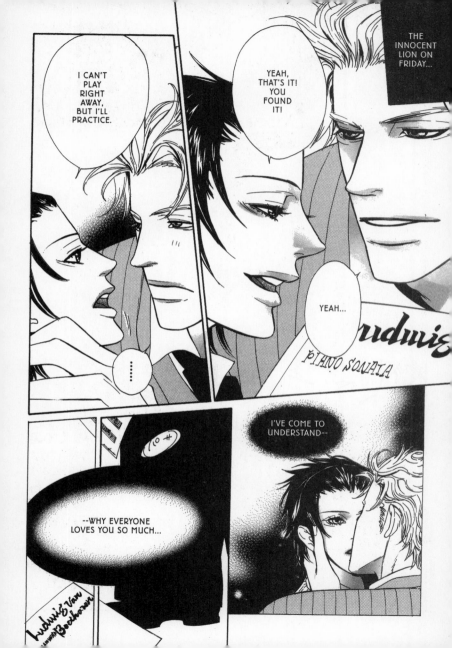

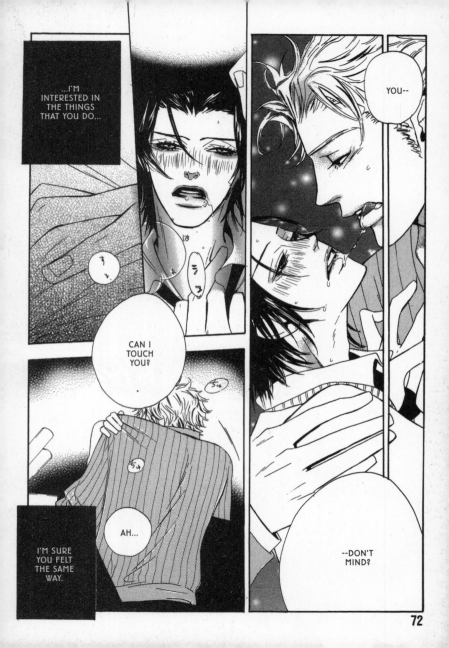

72

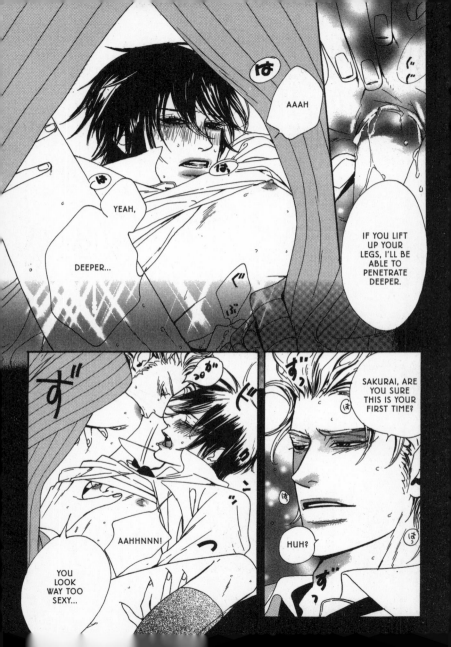

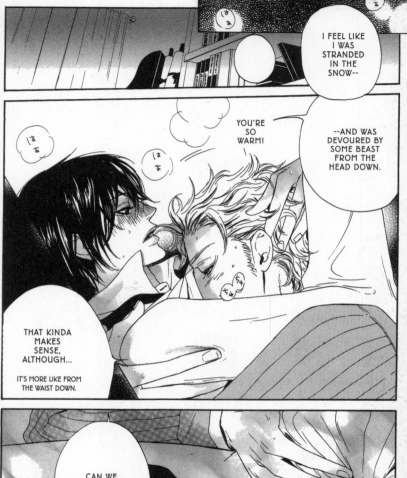
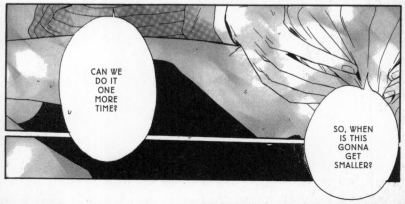

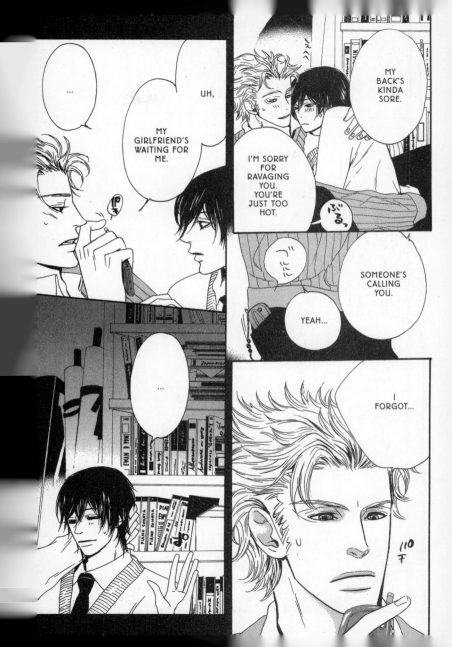

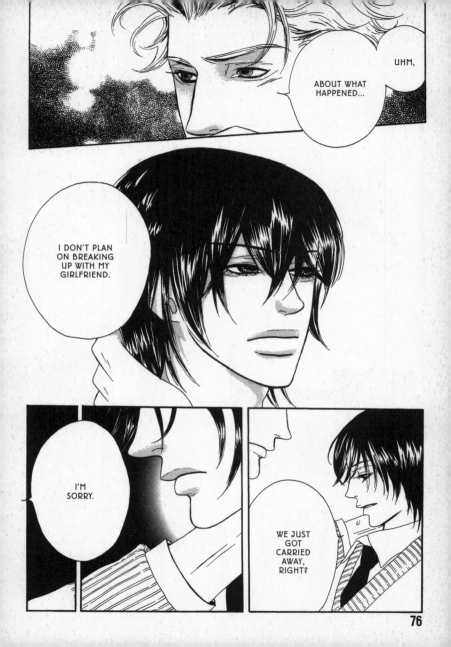

76

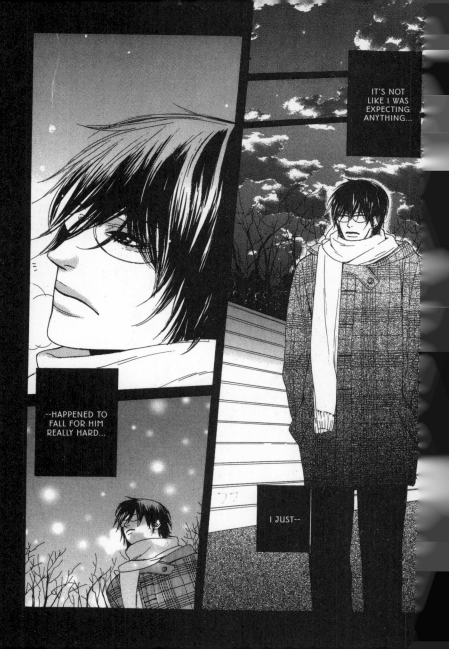

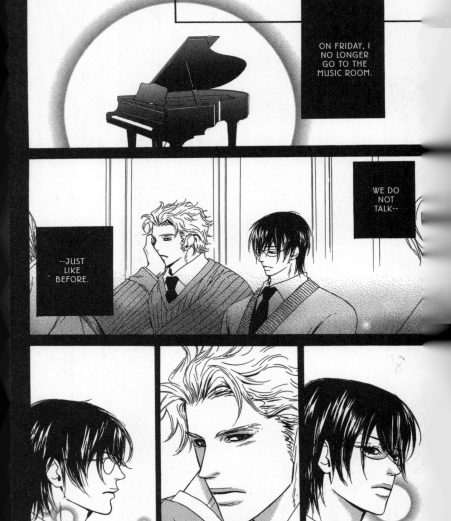

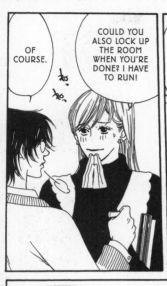

OF COURSE.

COULD YOU ALSO LOCK UP THE ROOM WHEN YOU'RE DONE? I HAVE TO RUN!

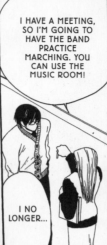

I HAVE A MEETING, SO I'M GOING TO HAVE THE BAND PRACTICE MARCHING. YOU CAN USE THE MUSIC ROOM!

I NO LONGER...

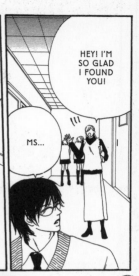

MS...

HEY! I'M SO GLAD I FOUND YOU!

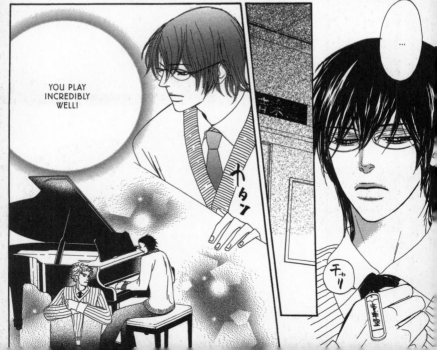

YOU PLAY INCREDIBLY WELL!

...

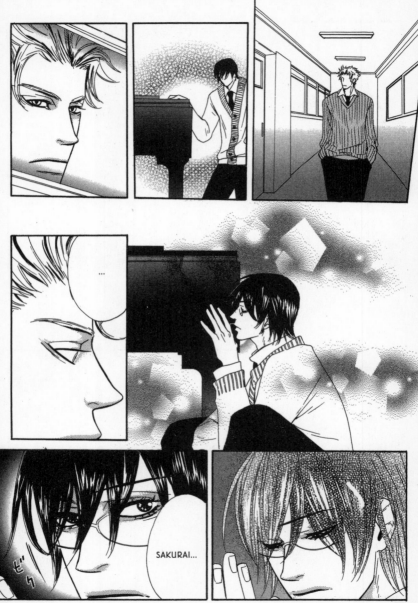

SAKURAI...

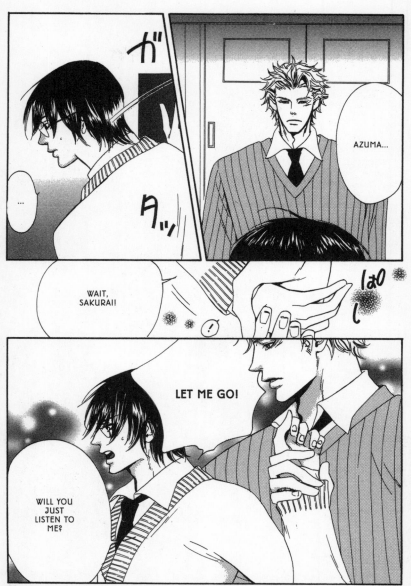

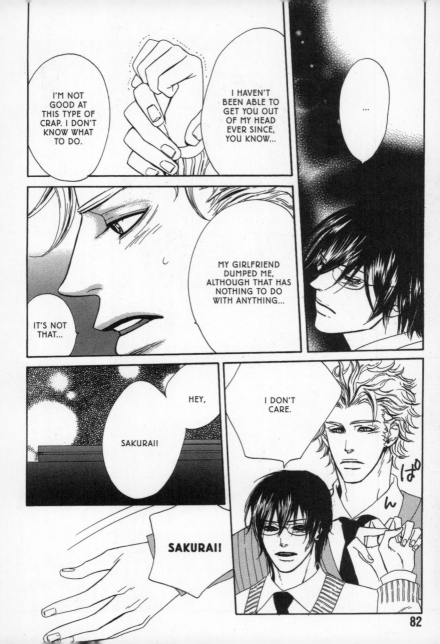

I'M NOT GOOD AT THIS TYPE OF CRAP. I DON'T KNOW WHAT TO DO.

I HAVEN'T BEEN ABLE TO GET YOU OUT OF MY HEAD EVER SINCE, YOU KNOW...

...

MY GIRLFRIEND DUMPED ME, ALTHOUGH THAT HAS NOTHING TO DO WITH ANYTHING...

IT'S NOT THAT...

HEY,

SAKURAI!

SAKURAI!

I DON'T CARE.

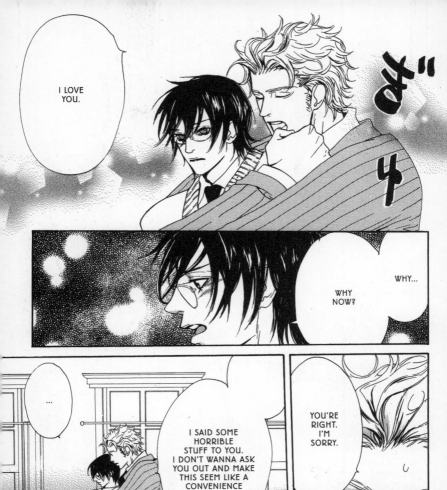

I LOVE YOU.

WHY...

WHY NOW?

...

I SAID SOME HORRIBLE STUFF TO YOU. I DON'T WANNA ASK YOU OUT AND MAKE THIS SEEM LIKE A CONVENIENCE FLING...

YOU'RE RIGHT. I'M SORRY.

I WANT YOU TO SMILE LIKE YOU USED TO.

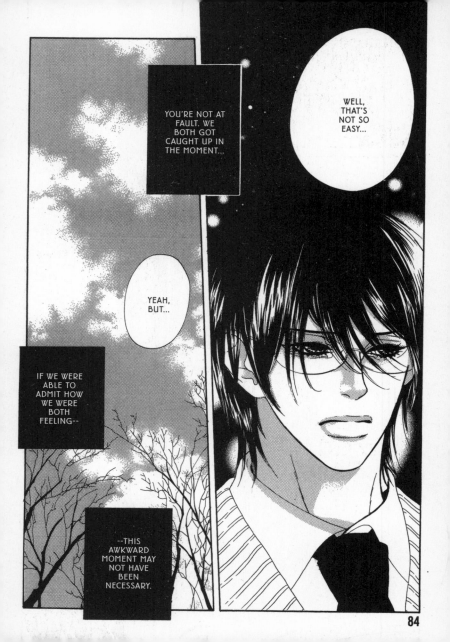

YOU'RE NOT AT FAULT. WE BOTH GOT CAUGHT UP IN THE MOMENT...

WELL, THAT'S NOT SO EASY...

YEAH, BUT...

IF WE WERE ABLE TO ADMIT HOW WE WERE BOTH FEELING--

--THIS AWKWARD MOMENT MAY NOT HAVE BEEN NECESSARY.

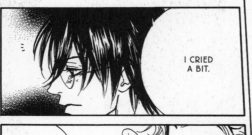

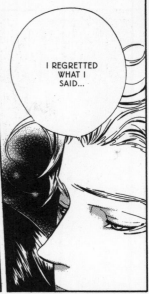

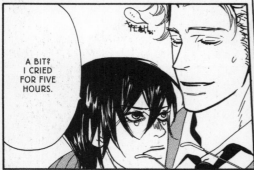

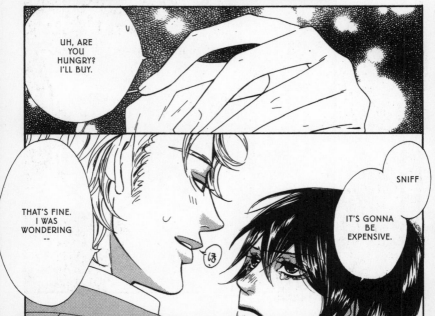

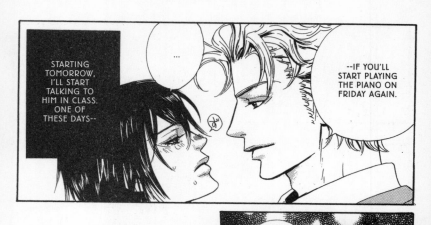

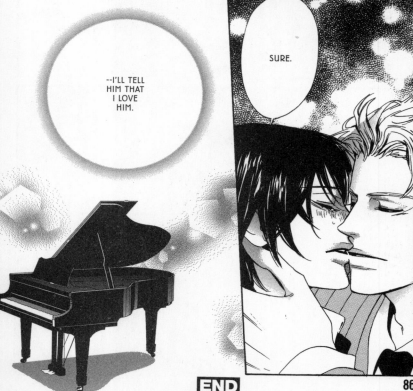

TROPICAL ECCENTRIC ASIA

LION ON FRIDAY EPISODE

IT WAS WINTERTIME. I GREW UP IN THE MOUNTAINS OF KYUSHU. TOKYO'S WINTER IS MUCH COLDER...

I'VE GOT THE HEATER ON. I'M FREEZING!

I KIND OF STOLE THE NAME, LION OF FRIDAY, FROM A SONG BY A TRIO.

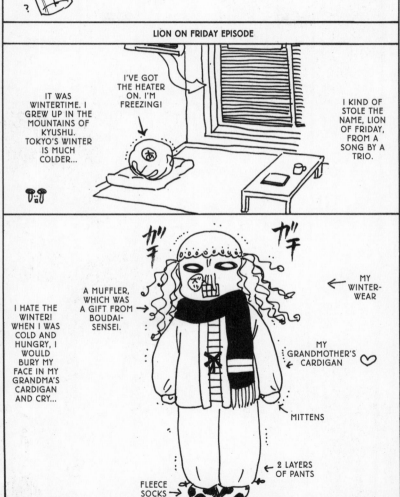

I HATE THE WINTER! WHEN I WAS COLD AND HUNGRY, I WOULD BURY MY FACE IN MY GRANDMA'S CARDIGAN AND CRY...

A MUFFLER, WHICH WAS A GIFT FROM BOUDAI-SENSEI.

MY WINTER-WEAR

MY GRANDMOTHER'S CARDIGAN

MITTENS

2 LAYERS OF PANTS

FLEECE SOCKS

Because I'm a Boy!

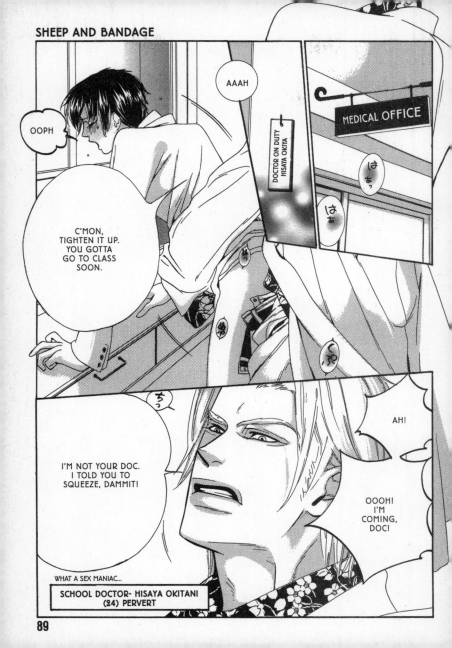

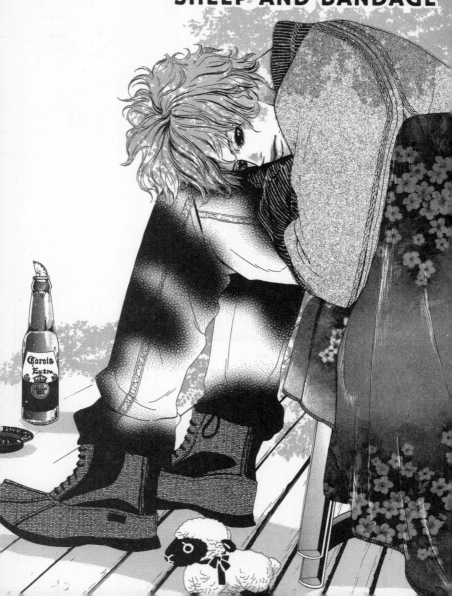

SHEEP AND BANDAGE

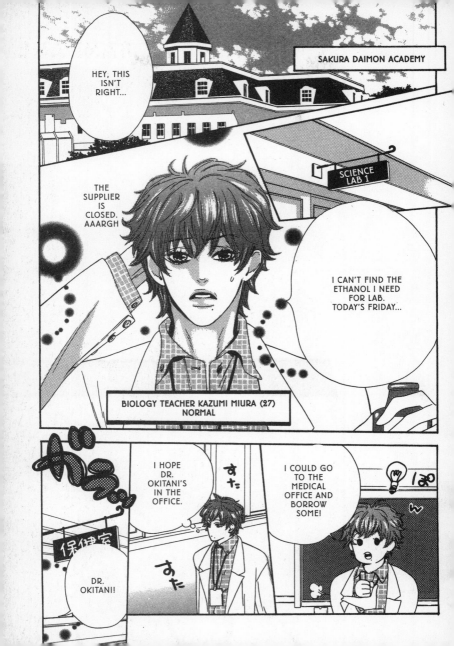

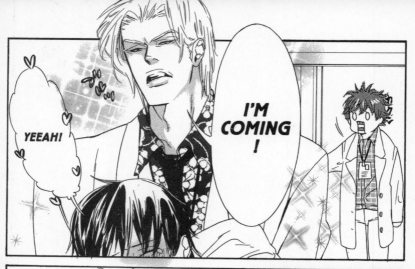

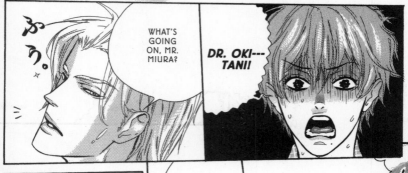

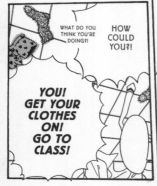

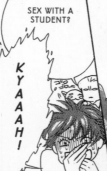

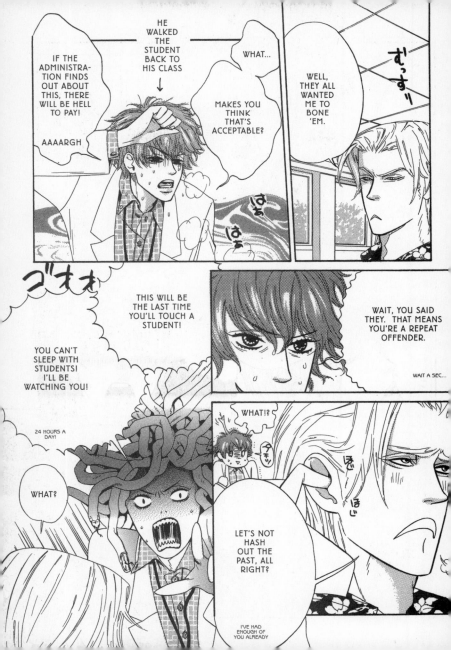

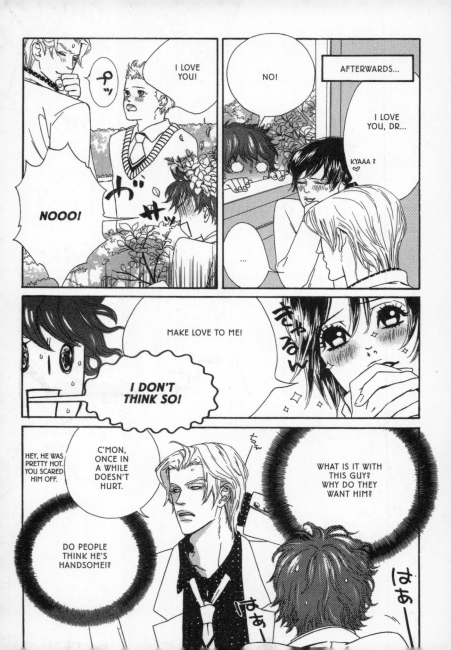

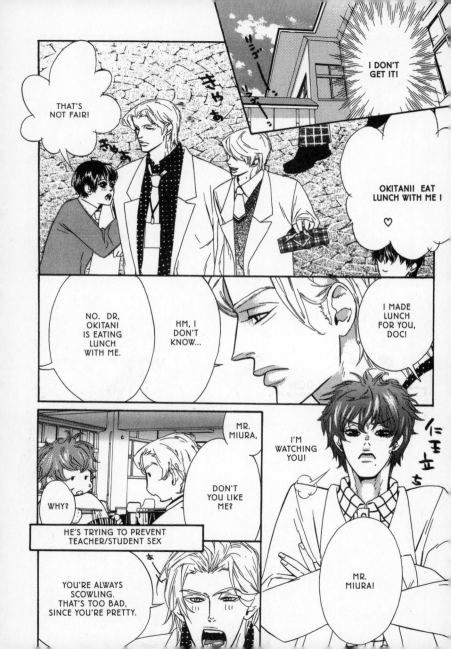

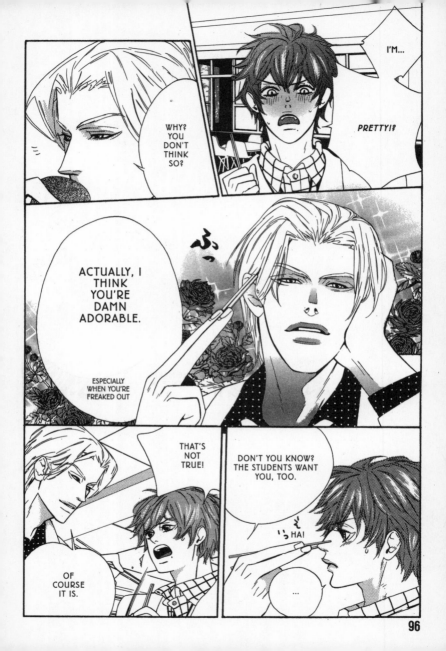

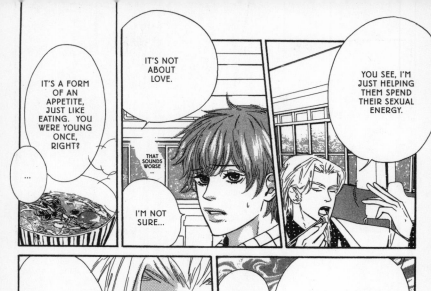

IT'S A FORM OF AN APPETITE, JUST LIKE EATING. YOU WERE YOUNG ONCE, RIGHT?

...

IT'S NOT ABOUT LOVE.

THAT SOUNDS WORSE...

I'M NOT SURE...

YOU SEE, I'M JUST HELPING THEM SPEND THEIR SEXUAL ENERGY.

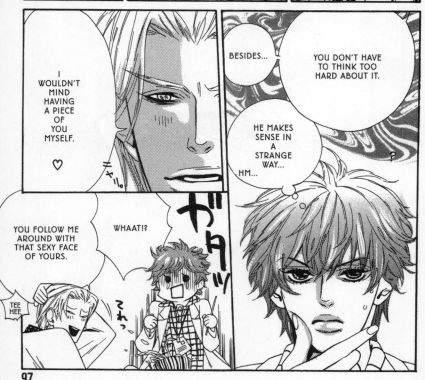

I WOULDN'T MIND HAVING A PIECE OF YOU MYSELF.

♡

BESIDES...

YOU DON'T HAVE TO THINK TOO HARD ABOUT IT.

HE MAKES SENSE IN A STRANGE WAY...

HM...

?

YOU FOLLOW ME AROUND WITH THAT SEXY FACE OF YOURS.

WHAAT!?

TEE HEE

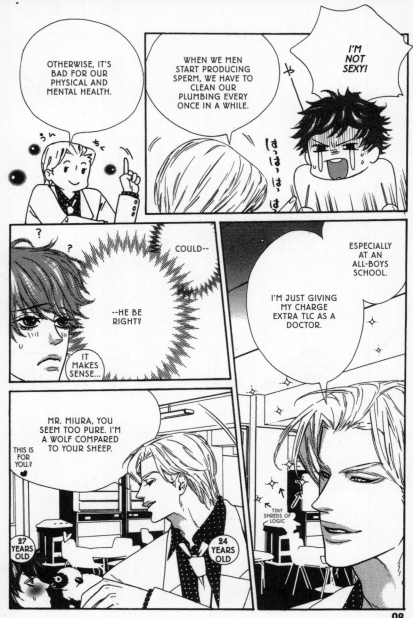

OTHERWISE, IT'S BAD FOR OUR PHYSICAL AND MENTAL HEALTH.

WHEN WE MEN START PRODUCING SPERM, WE HAVE TO CLEAN OUR PLUMBING EVERY ONCE IN A WHILE.

I'M NOT SEXY!

COULD--

--HE BE RIGHT?

IT MAKES SENSE...

ESPECIALLY AT AN ALL-BOYS SCHOOL.

I'M JUST GIVING MY CHARGE EXTRA TLC AS A DOCTOR.

MR. MIURA, YOU SEEM TOO PURE. I'M A WOLF COMPARED TO YOUR SHEEP.

THIS IS FOR YOU.?

27 YEARS OLD

24 YEARS OLD

← TINY SHREDS OF LOGIC

98

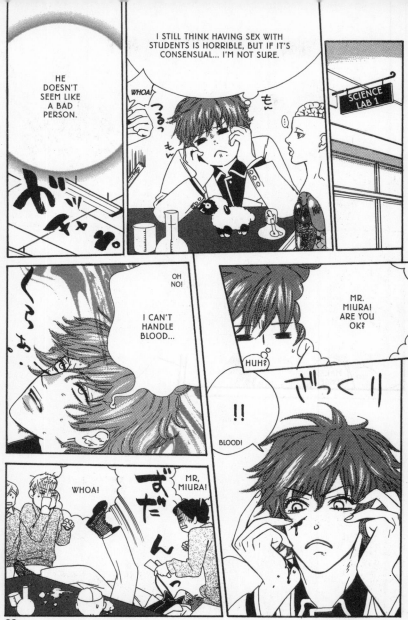

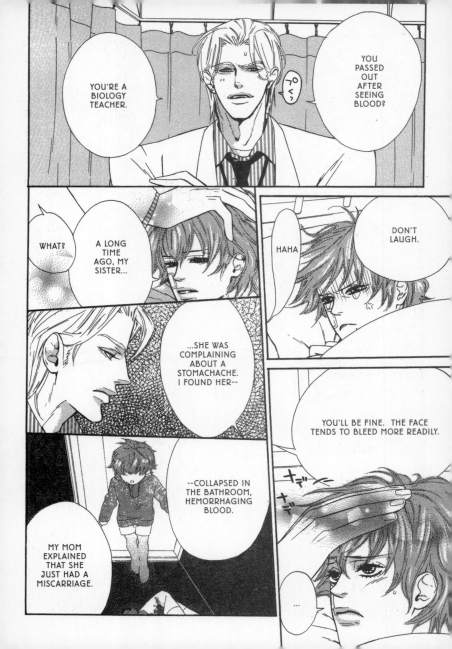

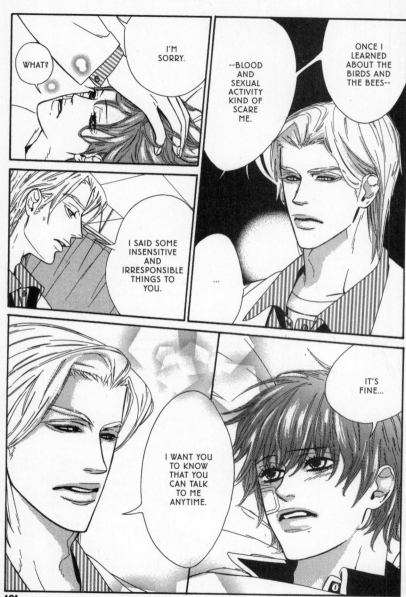

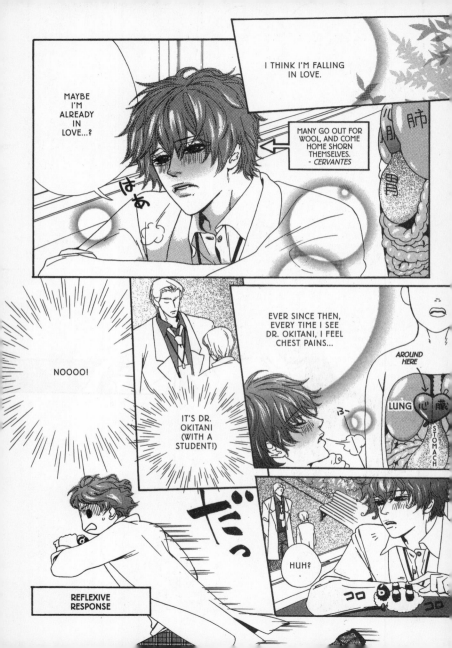

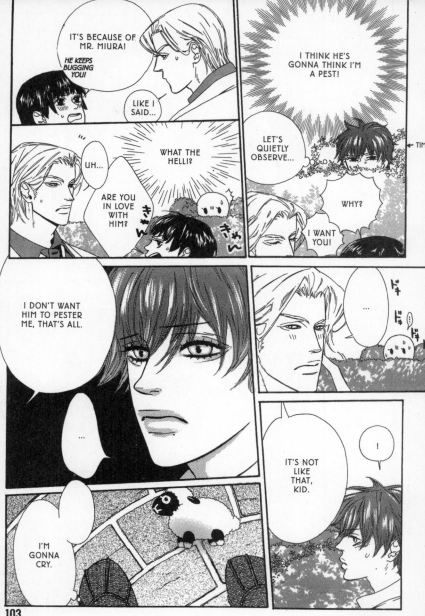

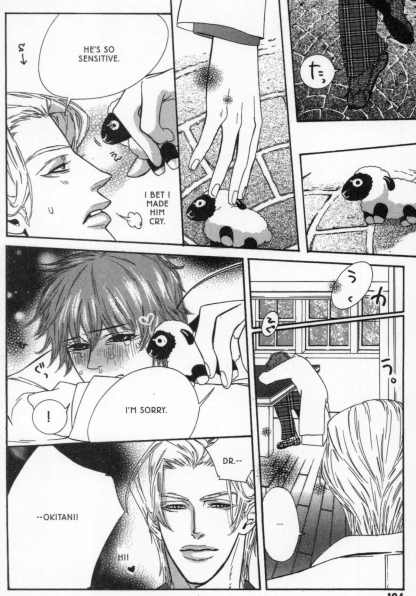

HE'S SO SENSITIVE.

I BET I MADE HIM CRY.

I'M SORRY.

!

DR.--

--OKITANI!!

HI!

...

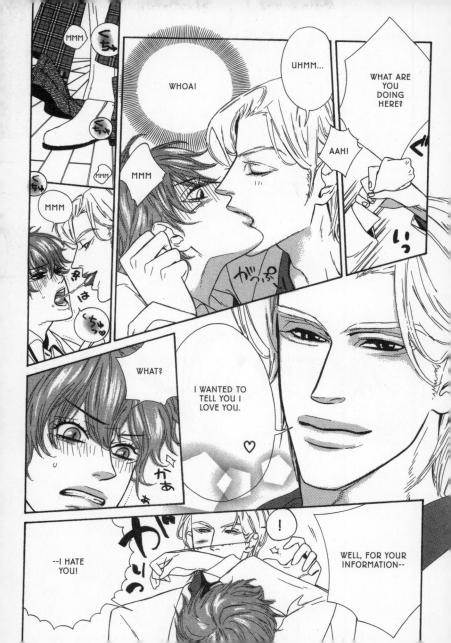

WHY ARE YOU DOING THIS TO ME?

YES?

UH...

HOW...?

YOU'RE AFRAID OF BLOOD AND SEX, BUT I CAN HELP YOU WITH THAT.

YOU'RE AFRAID BECAUSE YOU DON'T KNOW HOW GOOD IT FEELS.

MR. MIURA, HAVE YOU EVER HEARD ABOUT SHOCK THERAPY?

TROPICAL ECCENTRIC ASIA

SHEEP AND BANDAGE EPISODE

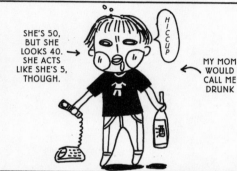

I DIDN'T HAVE ANY REFERENCE FOR INTERNAL ORGANS, SO I MADE A REALLY SIMPLE DRAWING...

♡

SHE'S 50, BUT SHE LOOKS 40. SHE ACTS LIKE SHE'S 5, THOUGH.

HICCUP

MY MOM WOULD CALL ME DRUNK

I WROTE THIS AFTER "LION ON FRIDAY." IT'S A DUMB STORY, BUT I HAD FUN WITH IT.

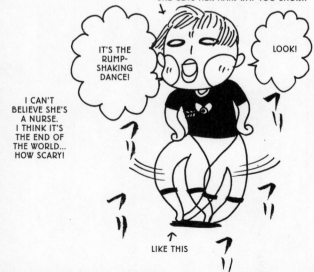

SHE CUTS HER HAIR WAY TOO SHORT.

IT'S THE RUMP-SHAKING DANCE!

LOOK!

I CAN'T BELIEVE SHE'S A NURSE. I THINK IT'S THE END OF THE WORLD... HOW SCARY!

I'M SUPPOSED TO BE PRETTY WEIRD (FROM WHAT PEOPLE TELL ME), BUT MY MOM IS WORSE.

LIKE THIS

Because I'm a Boy!

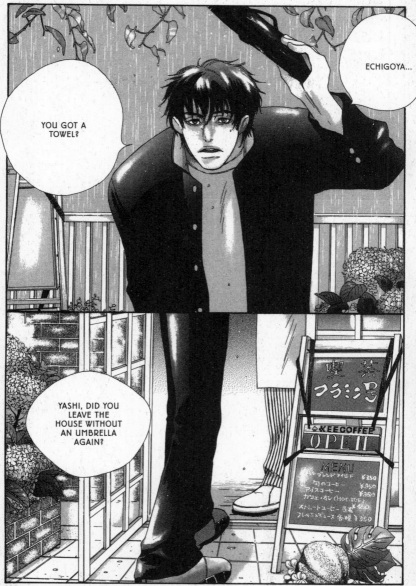

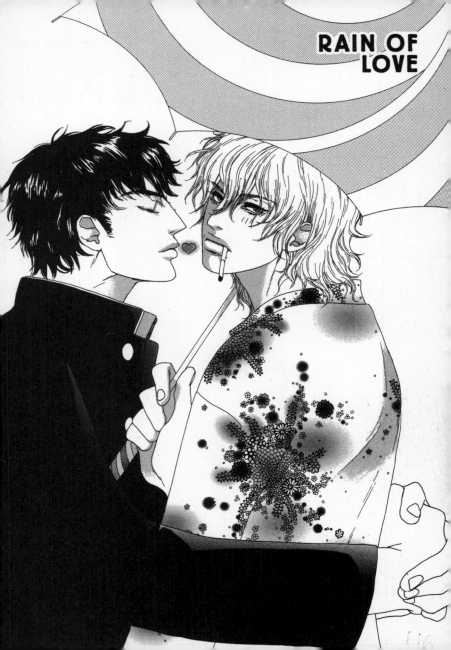

RAIN OF
LOVE

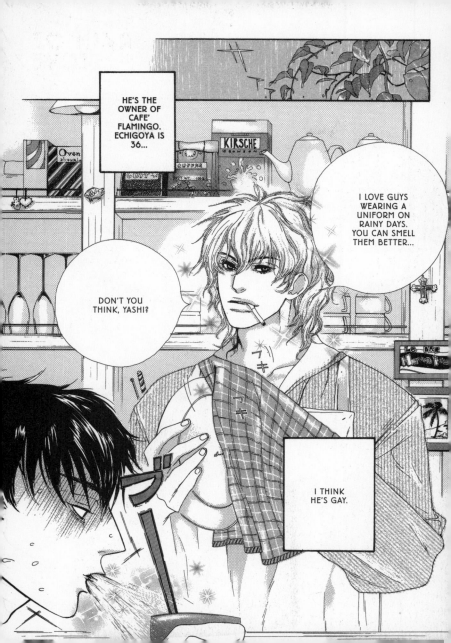

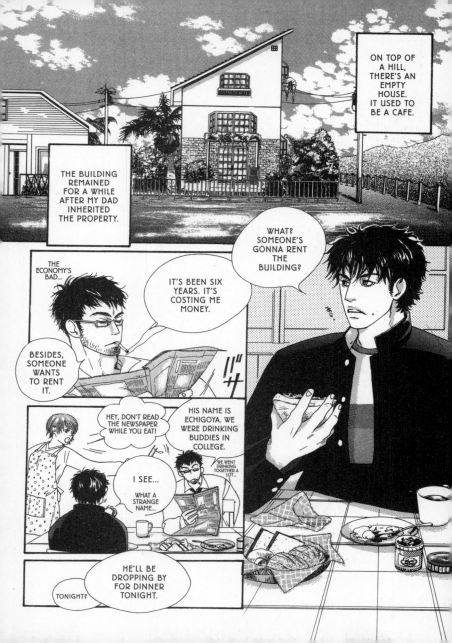

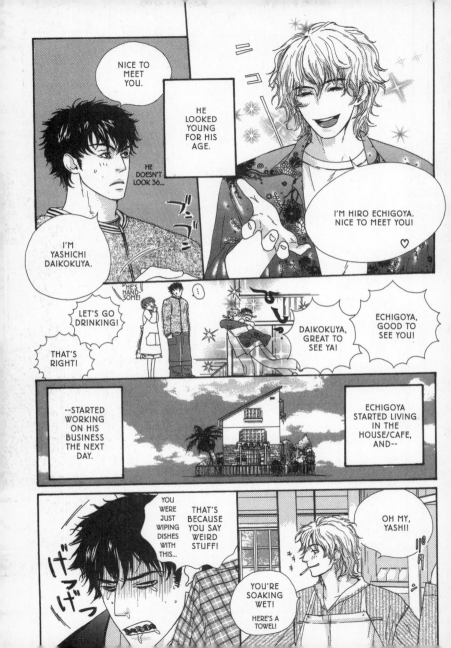

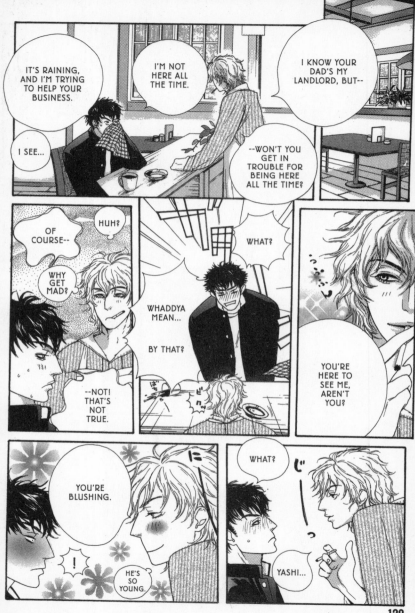

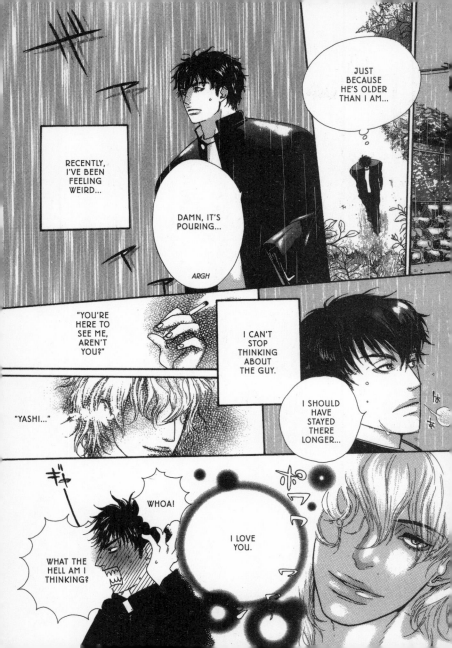

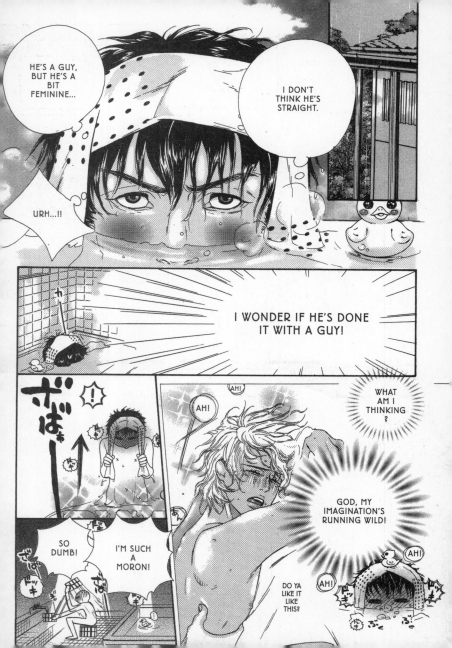

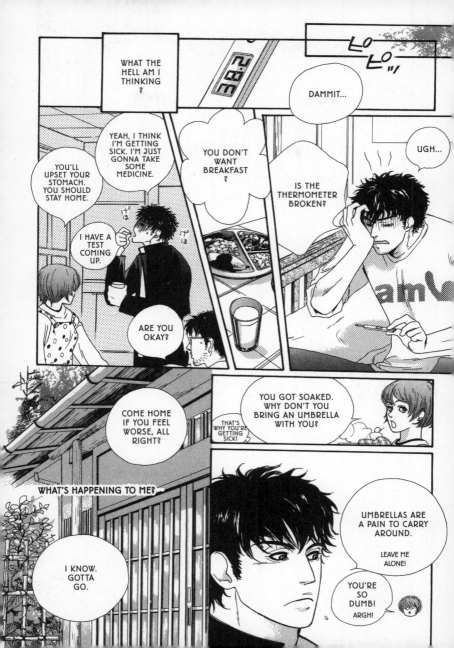

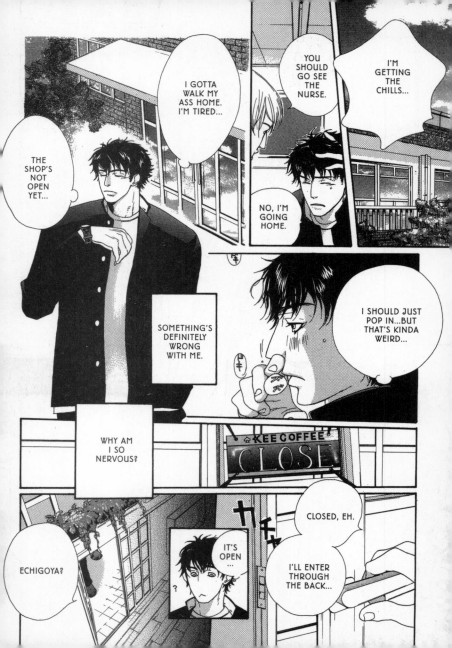

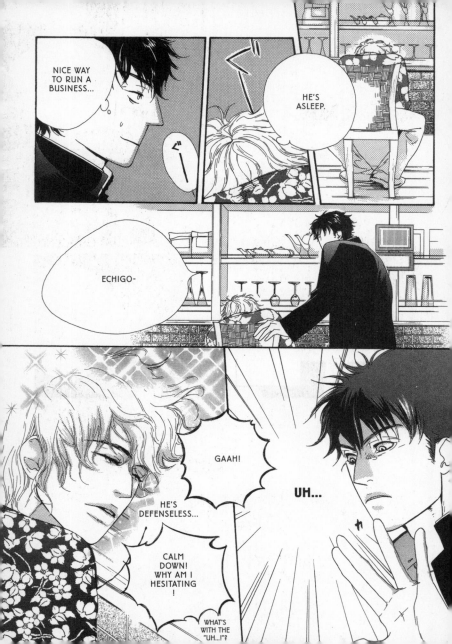

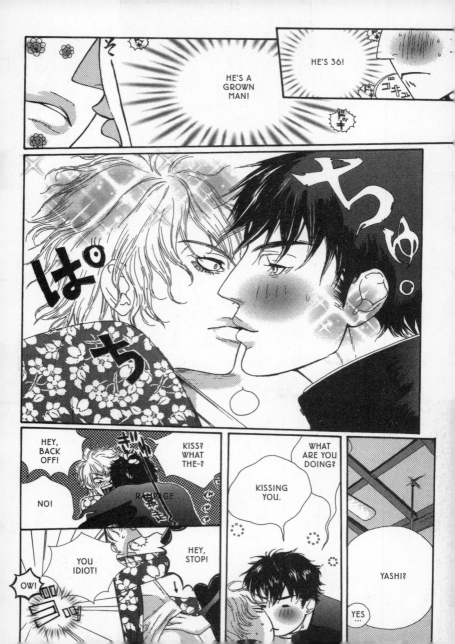

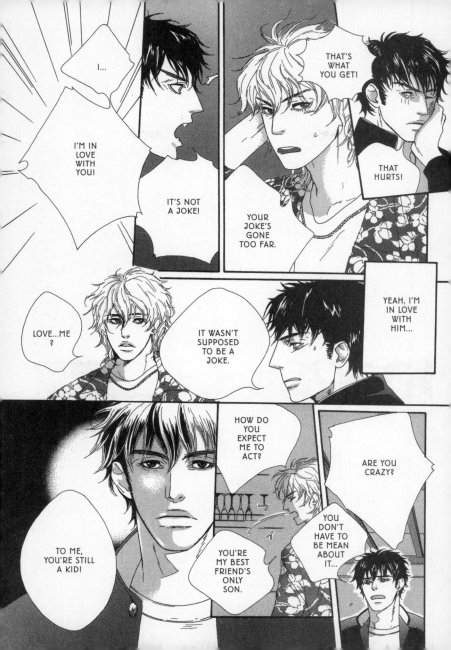

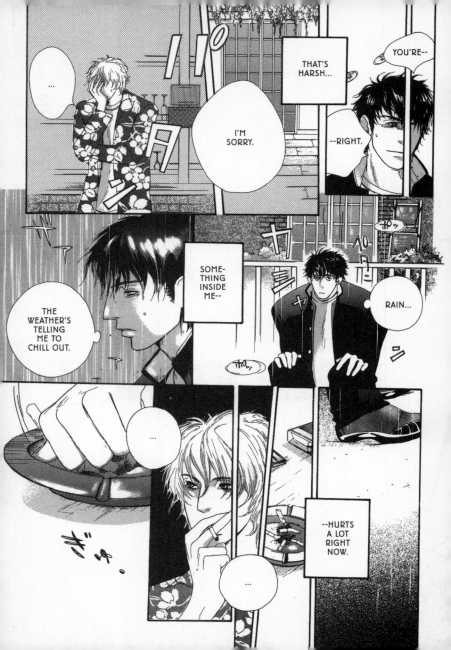

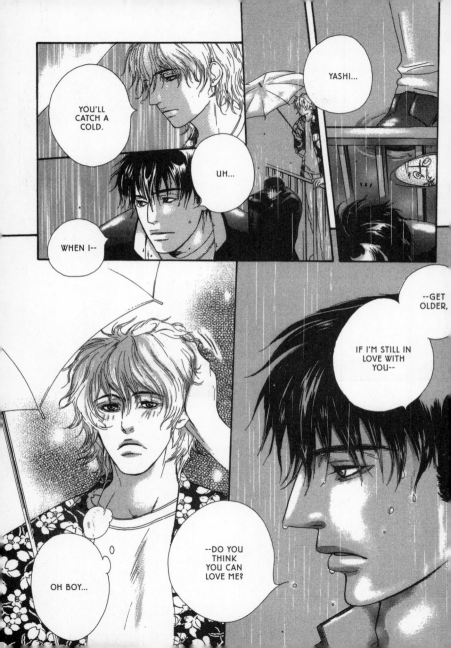

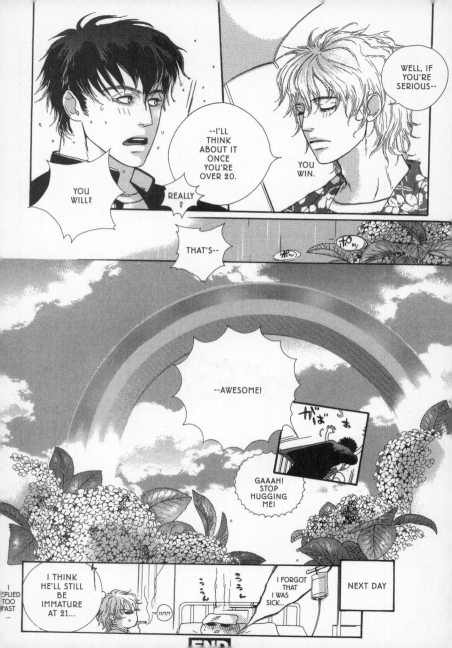

TROPICAL ECCENTRIC ASIA

RAIN OF LOVE EPISODE

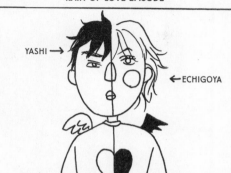

THE CHARACTERS ALL HAVE BIG NOSES. I HAVEN'T RETOUCHED ANYTHING BECAUSE OF ALL THE SCREENTONE (LAUGHS)

YASHI →

← ECHIGOYA

THIS IS A DEBUT PIECE. I USED WAY TOO MUCH SCREEN TONE...

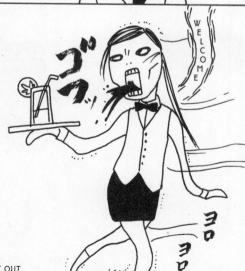

IT WAS REALLY, REALLY ROUGH.

WHEN I WAS WORKING ON THIS, I WAS WORKING AT A HOTEL AND AS A MANGA ASSISTANT.

I USED TO TAKE IT OUT ON THE CUSTOMERS.

Because I'm a Boy!

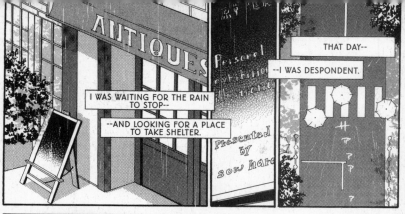

THAT DAY--

--I WAS DESPONDENT.

I WAS WAITING FOR THE RAIN TO STOP--

--AND LOOKING FOR A PLACE TO TAKE SHELTER.

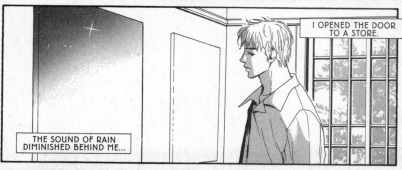

I OPENED THE DOOR TO A STORE.

THE SOUND OF RAIN DIMINISHED BEHIND ME...

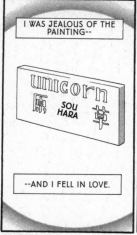

I WAS JEALOUS OF THE PAINTING--

--AND I FELL IN LOVE.

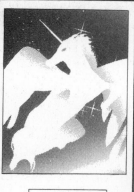

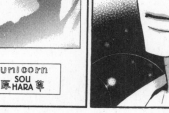

INSIDE THE EMPTY ROOM--

SHOW ME

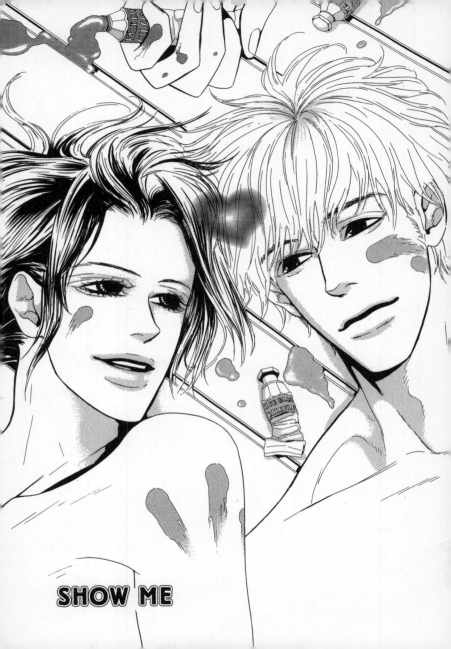

SHOW ME

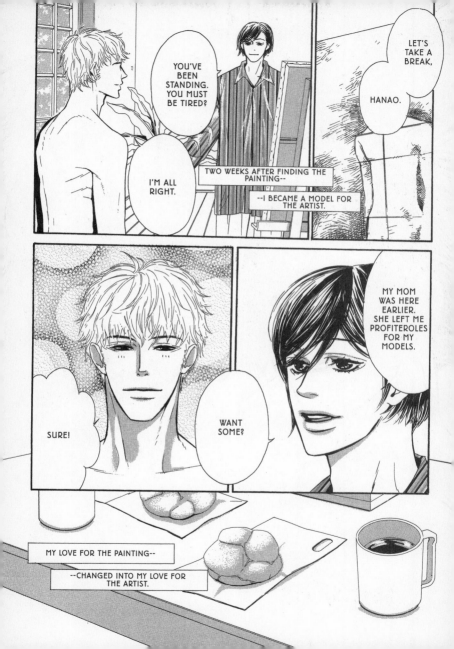

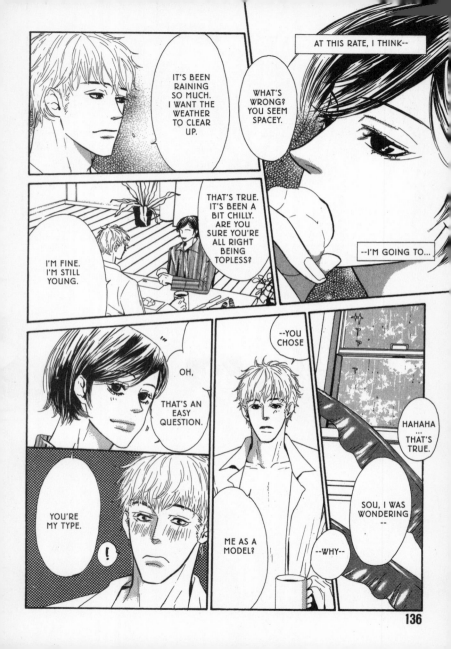

AT THIS RATE, I THINK--

IT'S BEEN RAINING SO MUCH. I WANT THE WEATHER TO CLEAR UP.

WHAT'S WRONG? YOU SEEM SPACEY.

--I'M GOING TO...

THAT'S TRUE. IT'S BEEN A BIT CHILLY. ARE YOU SURE YOU'RE ALL RIGHT BEING TOPLESS?

I'M FINE. I'M STILL YOUNG.

OH, THAT'S AN EASY QUESTION.

--YOU CHOSE

HAHAHA... THAT'S TRUE.

SOU, I WAS WONDERING --

YOU'RE MY TYPE.

ME AS A MODEL?

--WHY--

136

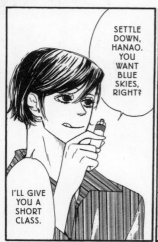

SETTLE DOWN, HANAO. YOU WANT BLUE SKIES, RIGHT?

I'LL GIVE YOU A SHORT CLASS.

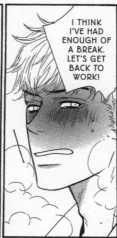

I THINK I'VE HAD ENOUGH OF A BREAK. LET'S GET BACK TO WORK!

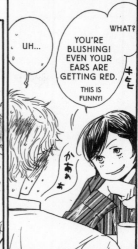

UH...

WHAT?

YOU'RE BLUSHING! EVEN YOUR EARS ARE GETTING RED.

THIS IS FUNNY!

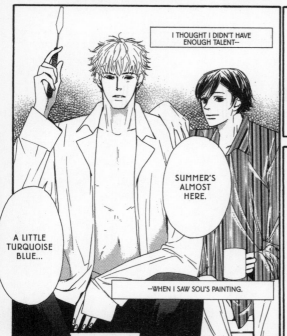

I THOUGHT I DIDN'T HAVE ENOUGH TALENT--

SUMMER'S ALMOST HERE.

A LITTLE TURQUOISE BLUE...

--WHEN I SAW SOU'S PAINTING.

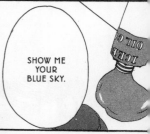

SHOW ME YOUR BLUE SKY.

ICE OIL C

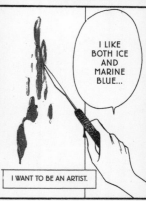

I LIKE BOTH ICE AND MARINE BLUE...

I WANT TO BE AN ARTIST.

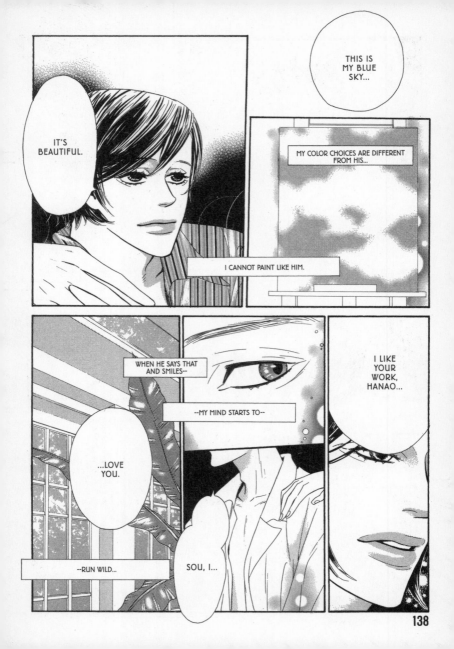

138

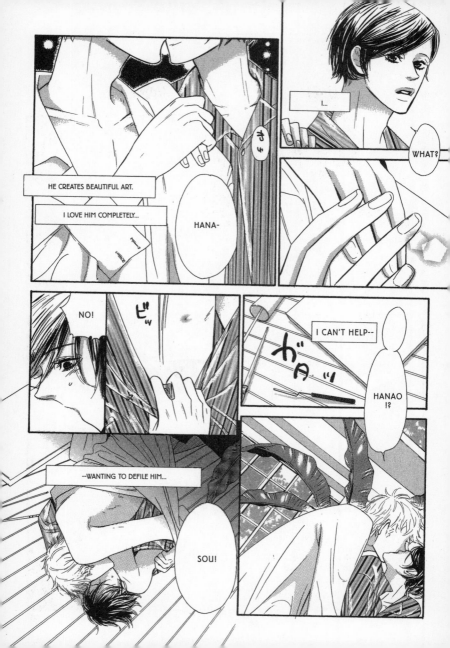

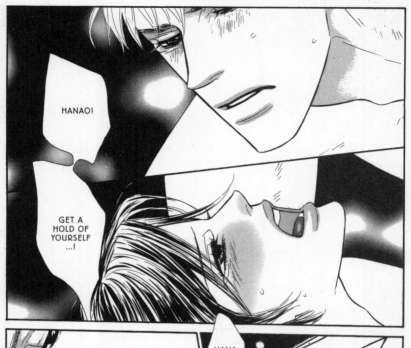

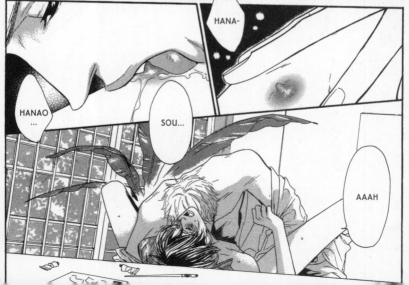

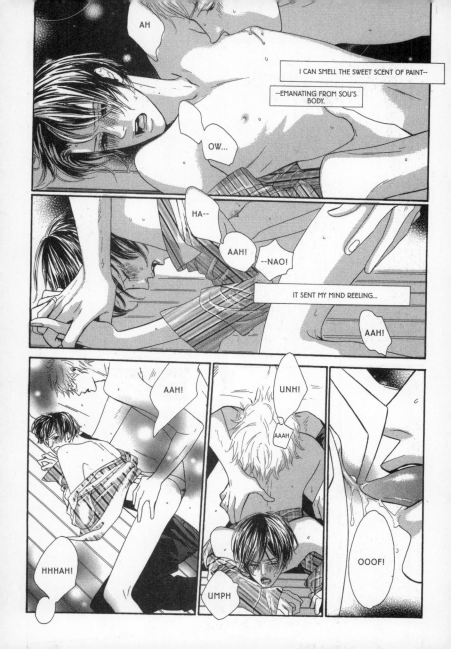

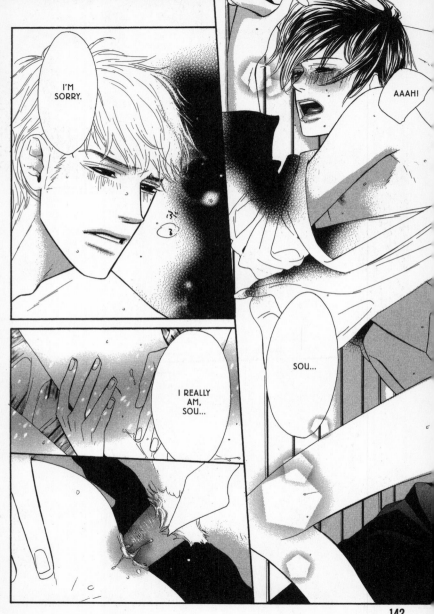

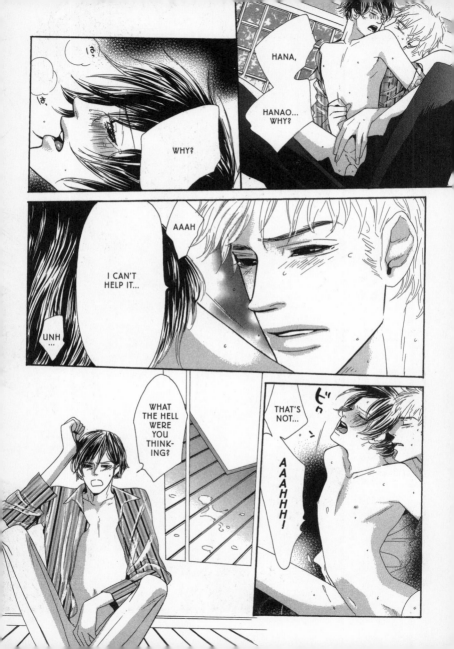

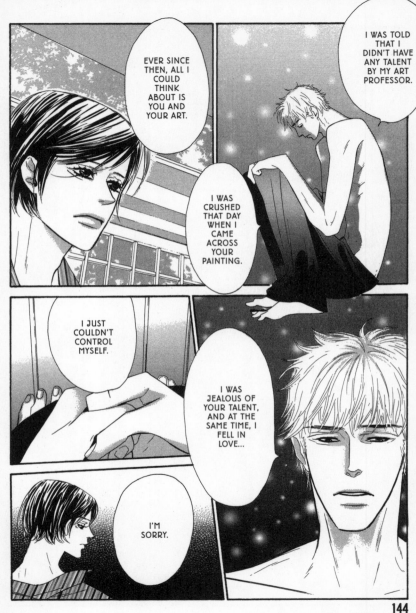

144

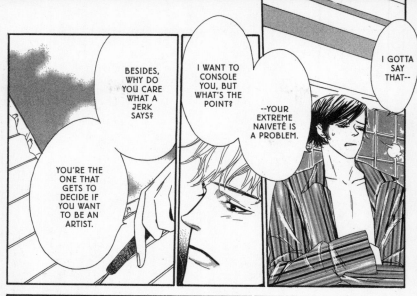

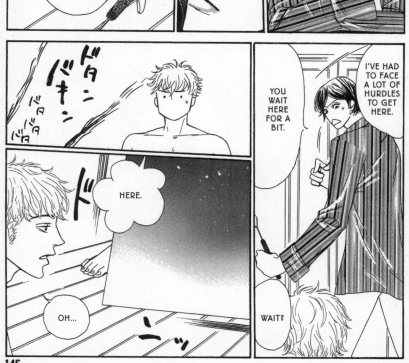

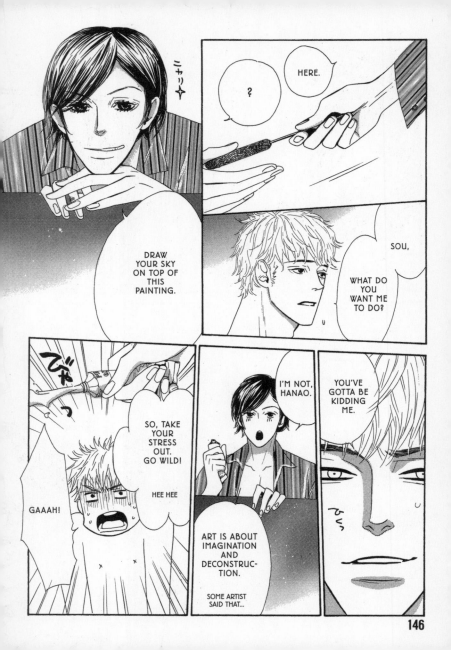

146

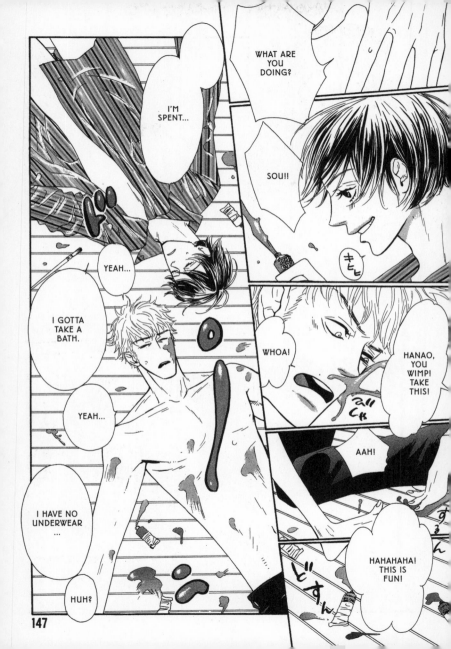

147

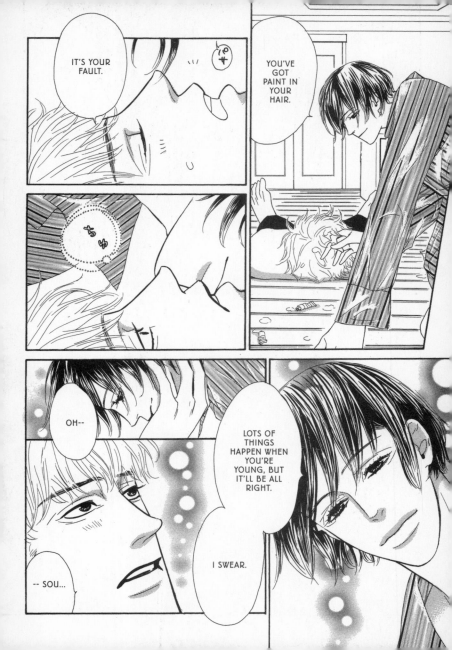

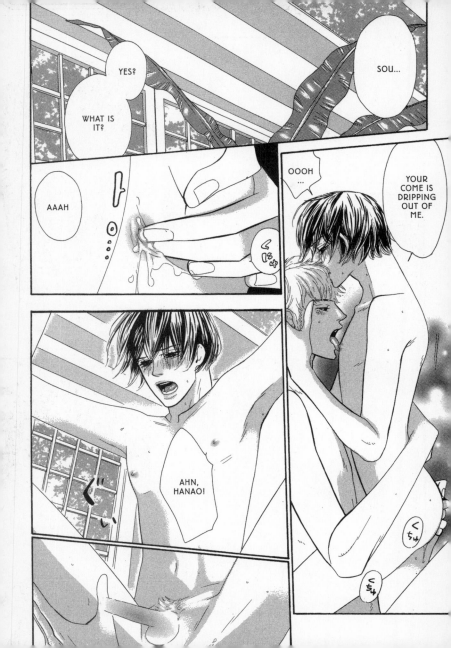

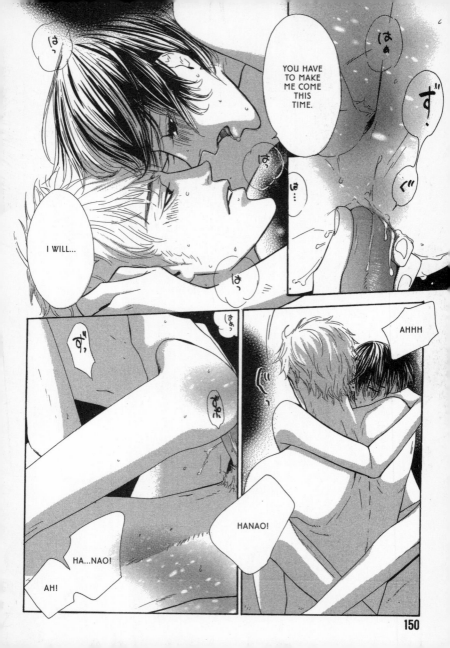

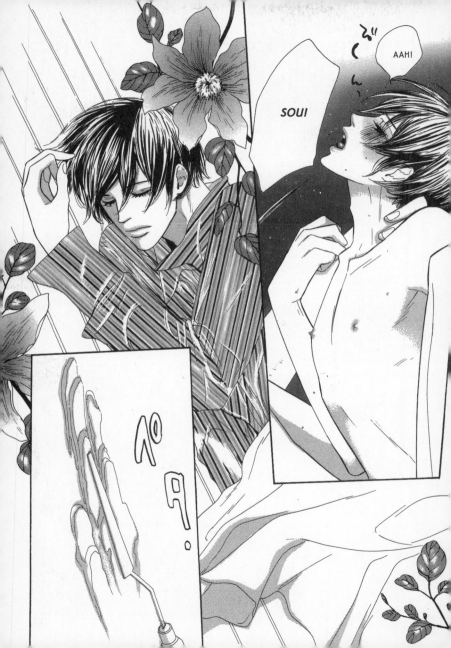

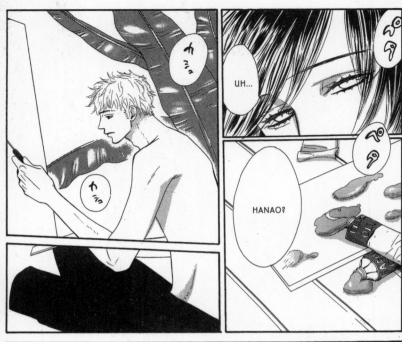

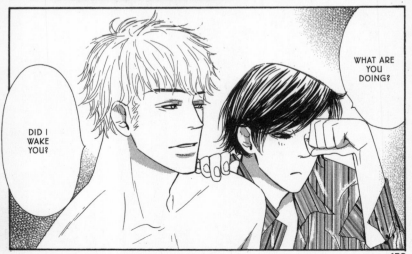

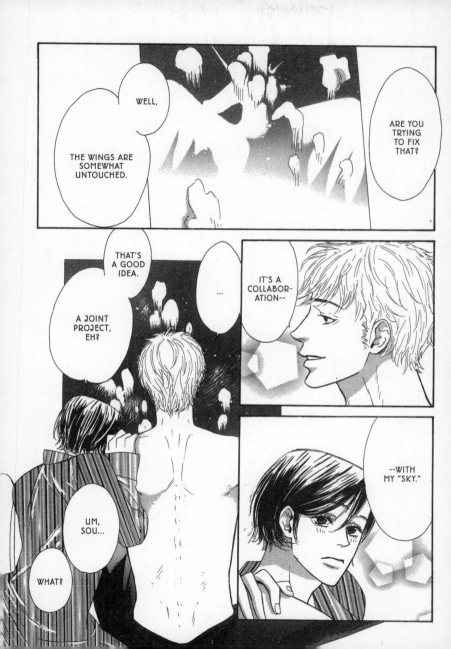

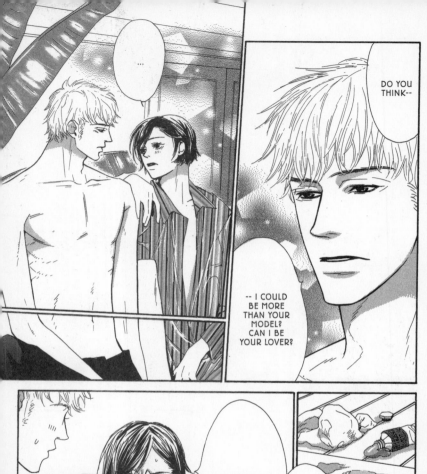

...

DO YOU THINK--

-- I COULD BE MORE THAN YOUR MODEL? CAN I BE YOUR LOVER?

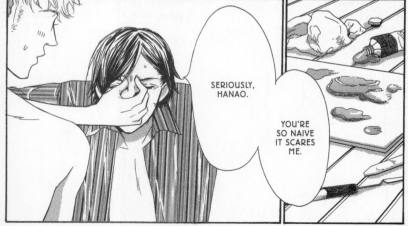

SERIOUSLY, HANAO.

YOU'RE SO NAIVE IT SCARES ME.

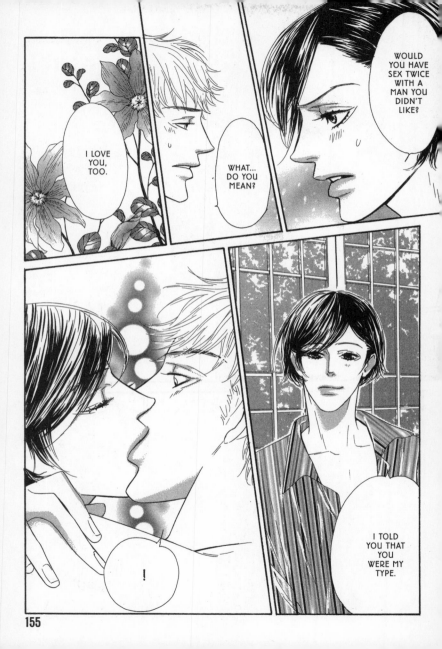

155

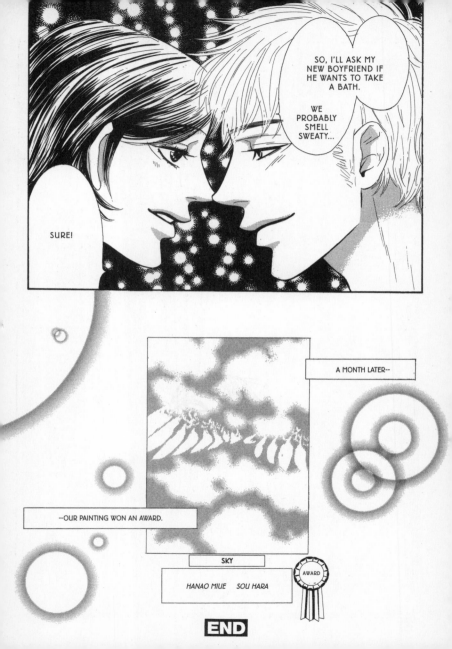

TROPICAL ECCENTRIC ASIA

SHOW ME EPISODE

SCHEDULE

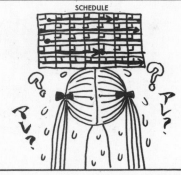

IN ONE MONTH, I HAD TO FINISH 80 PAGES TOTAL.

THIS ISN'T GOOD... I WAS HAPPY THAT I WAS GETTING WORK FROM OTHER COMPANIES, BUT, WHAT A MESS...

I'M GOING TO DIE! DIE!

I GOT A NOSEBLEED FROM THE STRESS...

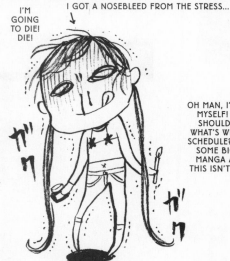

I DID IT, THOUGH, ALMOST ALL BY MYSELF. I TOLD MY ASSISTANT LIKE IT WAS NO BIG DEAL...

I'M SUCH AN IDIOT!

OH MAN, I'M ALL BY MYSELF! WHAT SHOULD I DO? WHAT'S WITH THIS SCHEDULE? I'M NOT SOME BIG-TIME MANGA ARTIST! THIS ISN'T RIGHT...

THIS IS THE REASON FOR THE STORY BEING SO NEGATIVE!

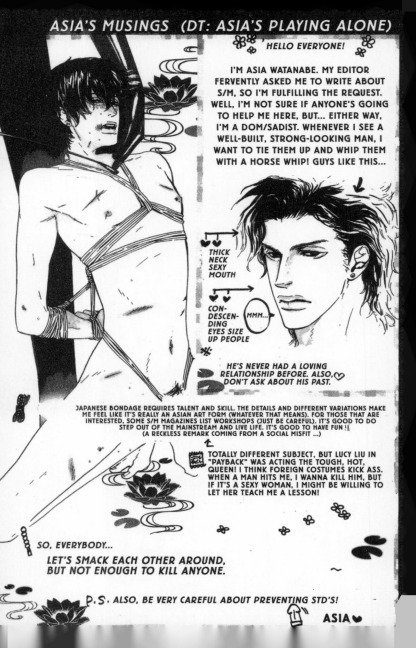

HELLO EVERYONE!

I'M ASIA WATANABE. MY EDITOR FERVENTLY ASKED ME TO WRITE ABOUT S/M, SO I'M FULFILLING THE REQUEST. WELL, I'M NOT SURE IF ANYONE'S GOING TO HELP ME HERE, BUT... EITHER WAY, I'M A DOM/SADIST. WHENEVER I SEE A WELL-BUILT, STRONG-LOOKING MAN, I WANT TO TIE THEM UP AND WHIP THEM WITH A HORSE WHIP! GUYS LIKE THIS...

THICK
NECK
SEXY
MOUTH

CON-
DESCEN-
DING
EYES SIZE
UP PEOPLE

MMM...

HE'S NEVER HAD A LOVING RELATIONSHIP BEFORE. ALSO, DON'T ASK ABOUT HIS PAST.

JAPANESE BONDAGE REQUIRES TALENT AND SKILL. THE DETAILS AND DIFFERENT VARIATIONS MAKE ME FEEL LIKE IT'S REALLY AN ASIAN ART FORM (WHATEVER THAT MEANS). FOR THOSE THAT ARE INTERESTED, SOME S/M MAGAZINES LIST WORKSHOPS (JUST BE CAREFUL). IT'S GOOD TO DO STEP OUT OF THE MAINSTREAM AND LIVE LIFE. IT'S GOOD TO HAVE FUN !
(A RECKLESS REMARK COMING FROM A SOCIAL MISFIT ...)

TOTALLY DIFFERENT SUBJECT, BUT LUCY LIU IN "PAYBACK" WAS ACTING THE TOUGH, HOT, QUEEN! I THINK FOREIGN COSTUMES KICK ASS. WHEN A MAN HITS ME, I WANNA KILL HIM, BUT IF IT'S A SEXY WOMAN, I MIGHT BE WILLING TO LET HER TEACH ME A LESSON!

SO, EVERYBODY...

LET'S SMACK EACH OTHER AROUND, BUT NOT ENOUGH TO KILL ANYONE.

P.S. ALSO, BE VERY CAREFUL ABOUT PREVENTING STD'S!

ASIA

CANDY AND WHIP

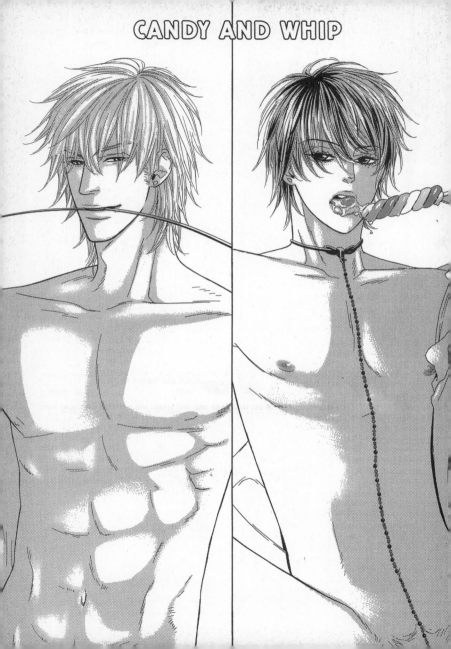

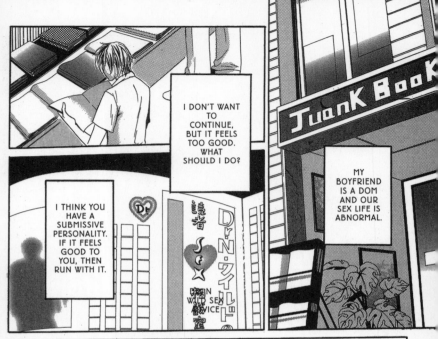

I DON'T WANT TO CONTINUE, BUT IT FEELS TOO GOOD. WHAT SHOULD I DO?

MY BOYFRIEND IS A DOM AND OUR SEX LIFE IS ABNORMAL.

I THINK YOU HAVE A SUBMISSIVE PERSONALITY. IF IT FEELS GOOD TO YOU, THEN RUN WITH IT.

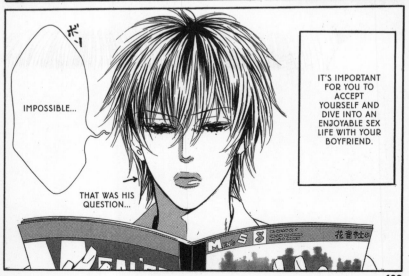

IT'S IMPORTANT FOR YOU TO ACCEPT YOURSELF AND DIVE INTO AN ENJOYABLE SEX LIFE WITH YOUR BOYFRIEND.

IMPOSSIBLE...

THAT WAS HIS QUESTION...

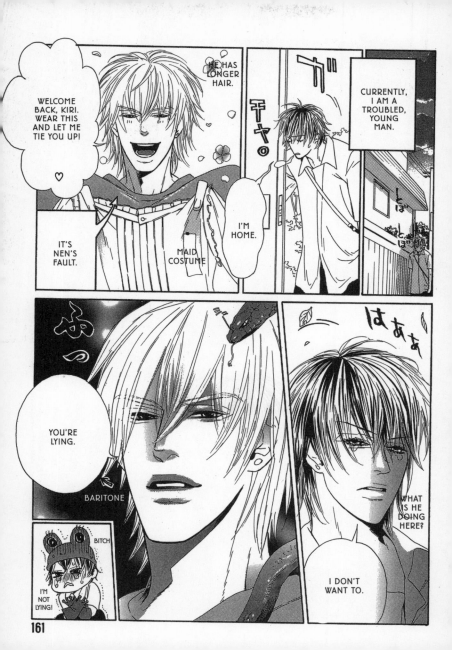

WELCOME BACK, KIRI. WEAR THIS AND LET ME TIE YOU UP!

HE HAS LONGER HAIR.

CURRENTLY, I AM A TROUBLED, YOUNG MAN.

IT'S NEN'S FAULT.

MAID COSTUME

I'M HOME.

YOU'RE LYING.

BARITONE

BITCH

I'M NOT LYING!

WHAT IS HE DOING HERE?

I DON'T WANT TO.

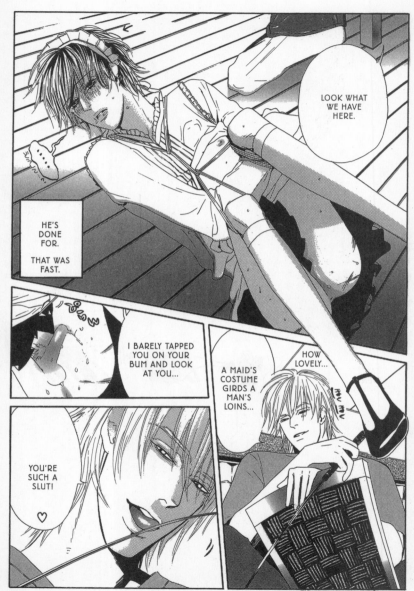

162

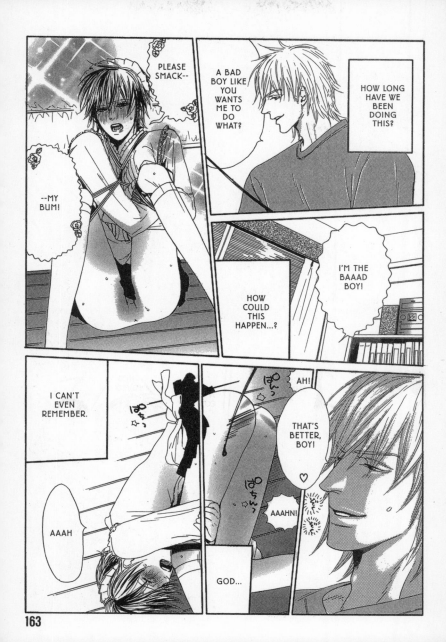

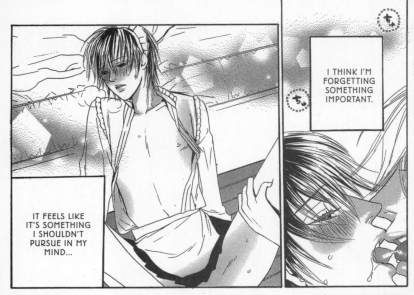

I THINK I'M FORGETTING SOMETHING IMPORTANT.

IT FEELS LIKE IT'S SOMETHING I SHOULDN'T PURSUE IN MY MIND...

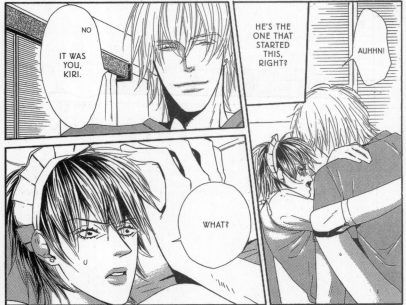

NO

IT WAS YOU, KIRI.

HE'S THE ONE THAT STARTED THIS, RIGHT?

AUHHN!

WHAT?

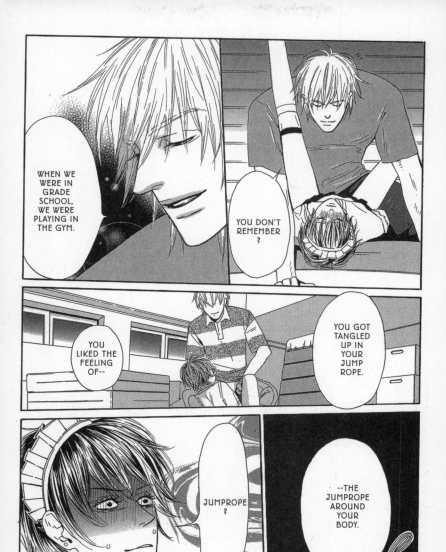

WHEN WE WERE IN GRADE SCHOOL, WE WERE PLAYING IN THE GYM.

YOU DON'T REMEMBER?

YOU LIKED THE FEELING OF--

YOU GOT TANGLED UP IN YOUR JUMP ROPE.

JUMPROPE?

--THE JUMPROPE AROUND YOUR BODY.

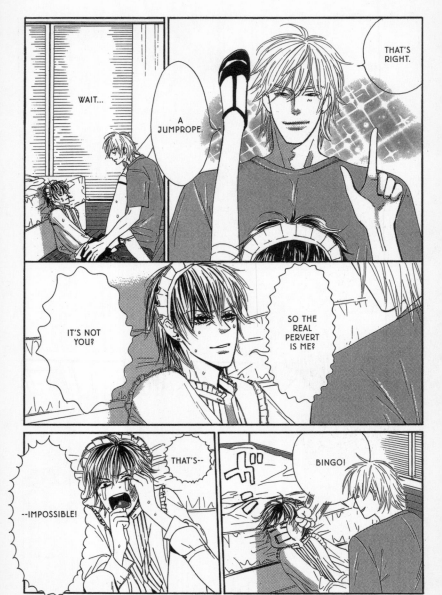

WAIT...

A JUMPROPE.

THAT'S RIGHT.

IT'S NOT YOU?

SO THE REAL PERVERT IS ME?

THAT'S--

--IMPOSSIBLE!

BINGO!

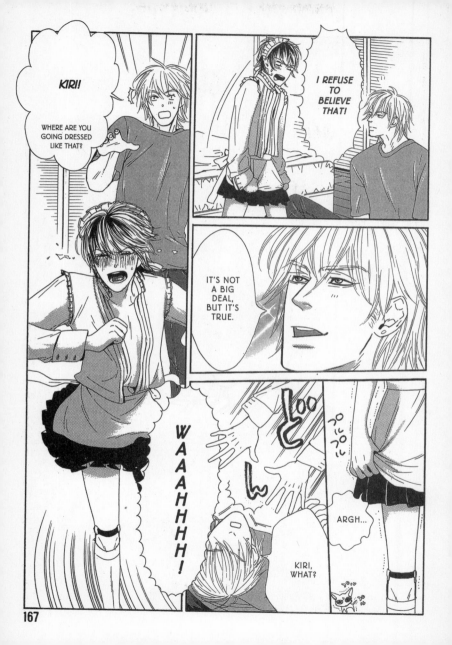

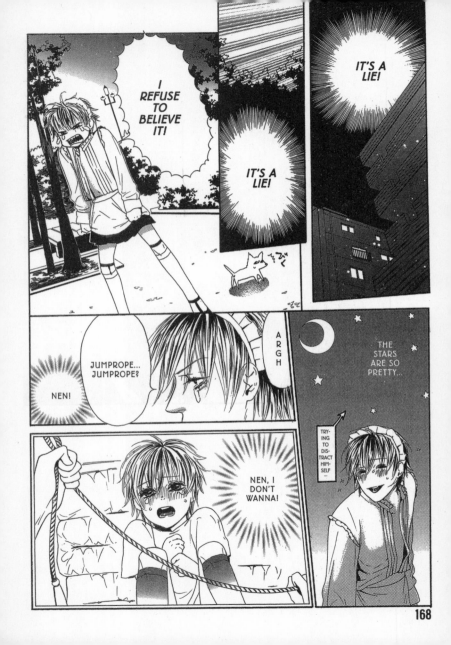

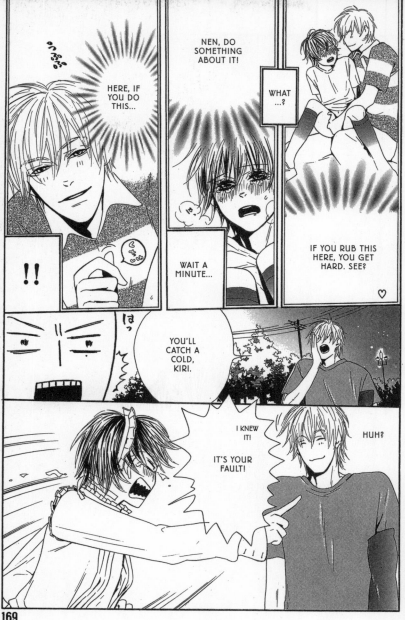

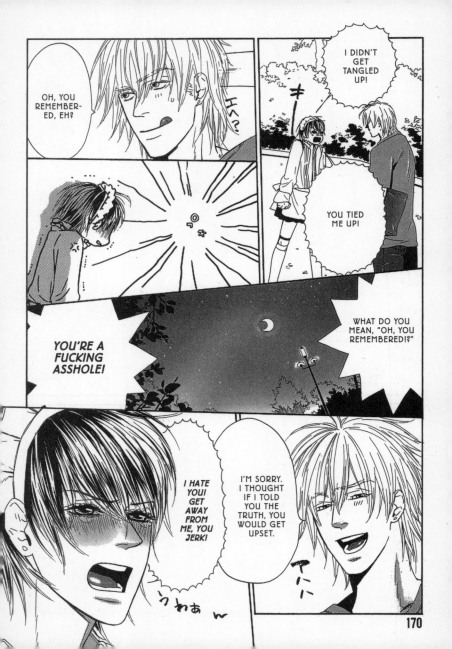

OH, YOU REMEMBER-ED, EH?

I DIDN'T GET TANGLED UP!

YOU TIED ME UP!

YOU'RE A FUCKING ASSHOLE!

WHAT DO YOU MEAN, "OH, YOU REMEMBERED!?"

I HATE YOU! GET AWAY FROM ME, YOU JERK!

I'M SORRY. I THOUGHT IF I TOLD YOU THE TRUTH, YOU WOULD GET UPSET.

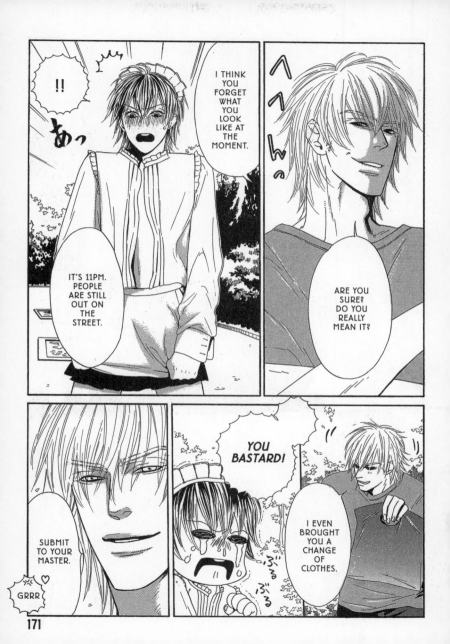

171

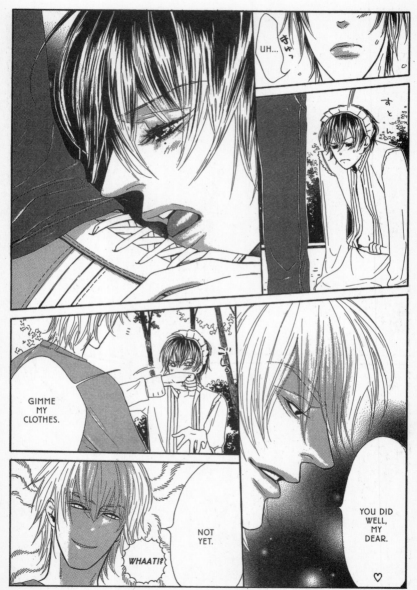

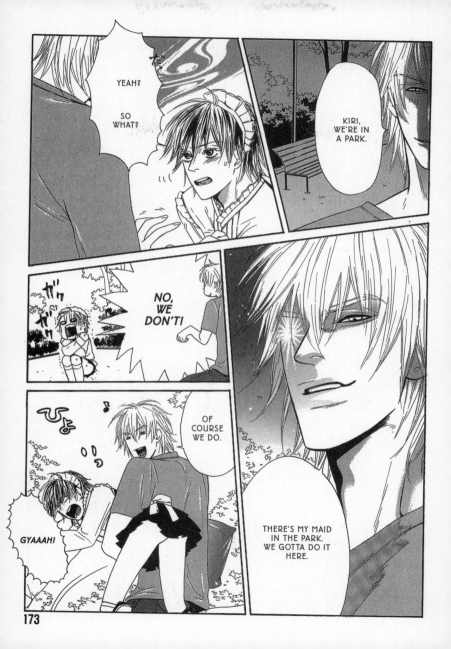

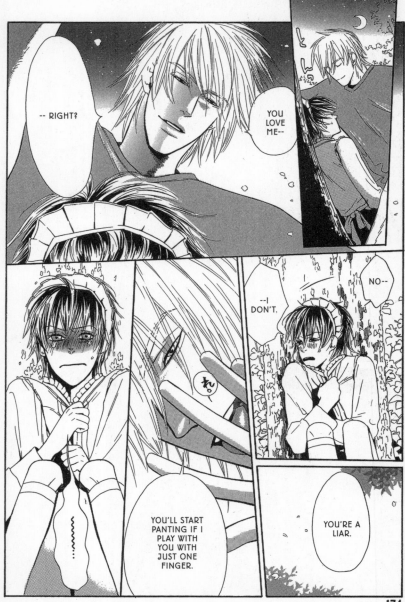

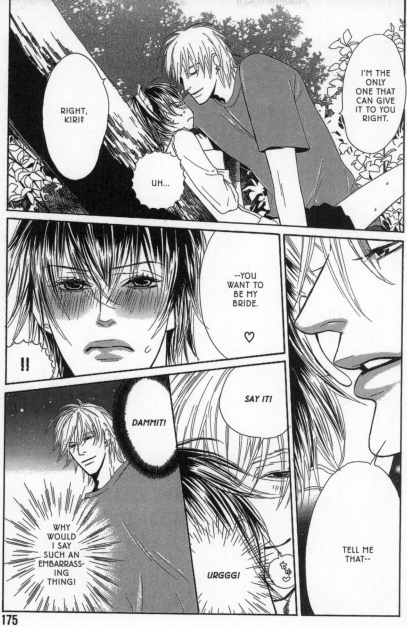

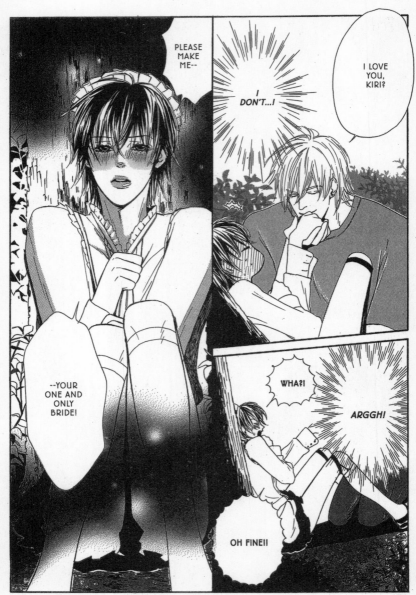

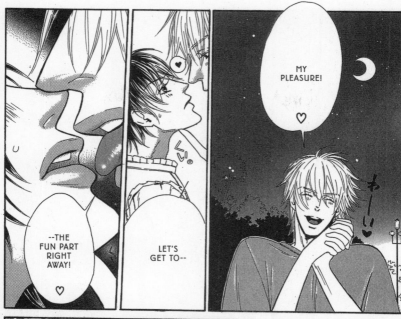

--THE FUN PART RIGHT AWAY! ♡

LET'S GET TO--

MY PLEASURE! ♡

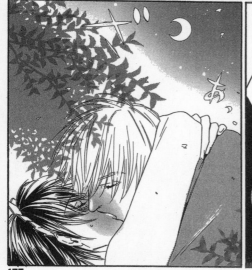

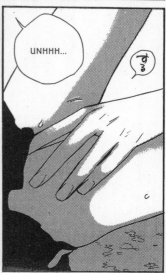

UNHHH...

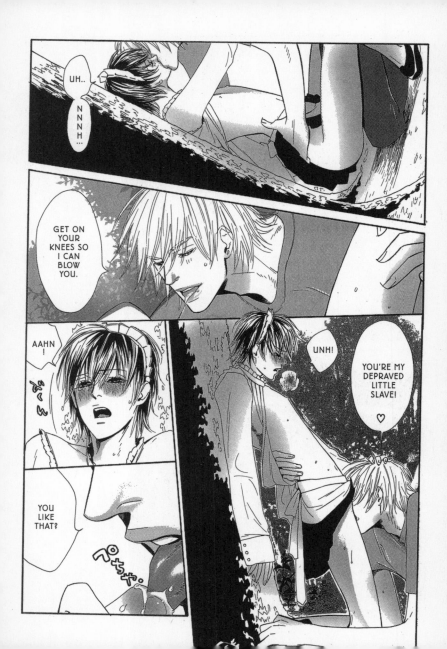

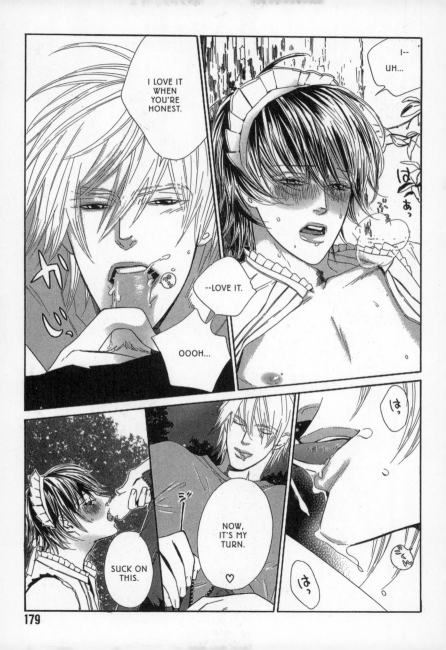

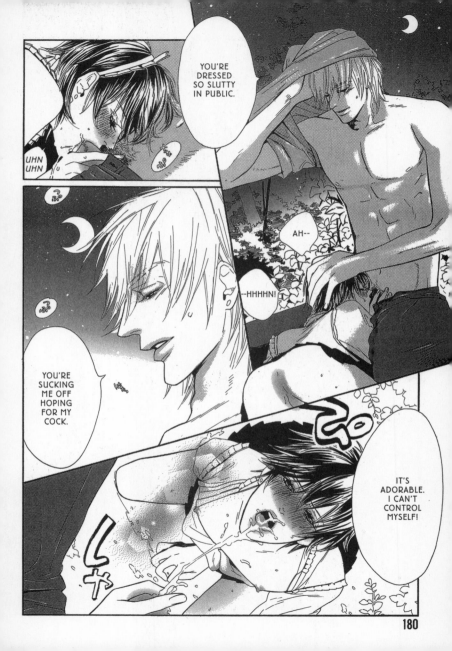

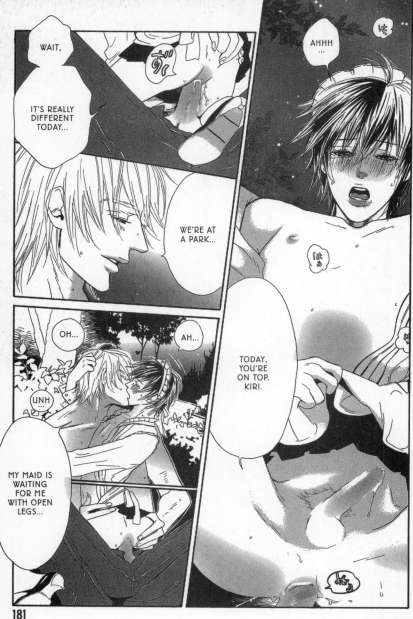

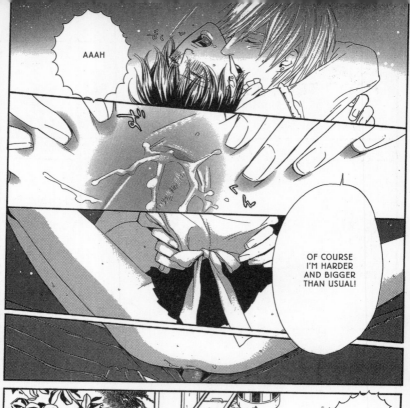

AAAH

OF COURSE I'M HARDER AND BIGGER THAN USUAL!

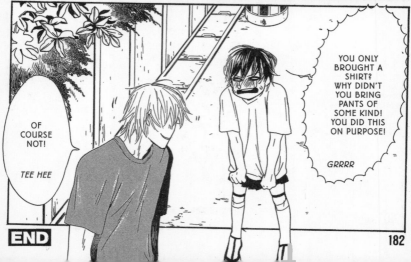

YOU ONLY BROUGHT A SHIRT? WHY DIDN'T YOU BRING PANTS OF SOME KIND! YOU DID THIS ON PURPOSE!

GRRRR

OF COURSE NOT!

TEE HEE

TROPICAL ECCENTRIC ASIA

THE FINAL CHAPTER

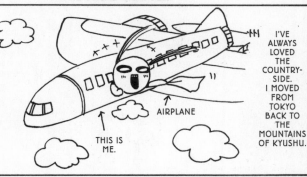

I WAS ONLY IN TOKYO FOR A LITTLE OVER 2 YEARS, BUT IT WAS REALLY STRESSFUL.

I'VE ALWAYS LOVED THE COUNTRY-SIDE. I MOVED FROM TOKYO BACK TO THE MOUNTAINS OF KYUSHU.

THIS IS ME.

AIRPLANE

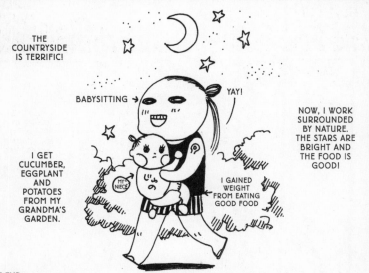

THE COUNTRYSIDE IS TERRIFIC!

BABYSITTING →

YAY!

NOW, I WORK SURROUNDED BY NATURE. THE STARS ARE BRIGHT AND THE FOOD IS GOOD!

I GET CUCUMBER, EGGPLANT AND POTATOES FROM MY GRANDMA'S GARDEN.

MY NIECE

I GAINED WEIGHT FROM EATING GOOD FOOD

THE END

❀ POSTSCRIPT ❀

UM, I'M AN AMATEUR, SO I'M NOT SURE WHAT I SHOULD WRITE.
FIRST AND FOREMOST, I WANT TO THANK ALL MY READERS.
I ALSO WANT TO THANK THE COURAGE OF MY EDITORS AND
PUBLISHERS THAT ALLOWED AN AMATEUR LIKE ME TO HAVE MY
OWN COMIC! THE GUIDANCE AND DELUSIONS OF MY EDITORS
ALLOWED ME TO FINALLY HAVE MY OWN COMIC...

THANK YOU SO MUCH!

I'D ALSO LIKE TO THANK MY READERS THAT WERE WILLING TO
PUT UP WITH MY NONSENSICAL STORIES, AND THOSE THAT
ACTUALLY BOUGHT THE DANG THING! I CAN'T SEE STRAIGHT
BECAUSE I'M CRYING! I'LL KEEP WORKING HARD TO MAINTAIN
YOUR LOYALTY!

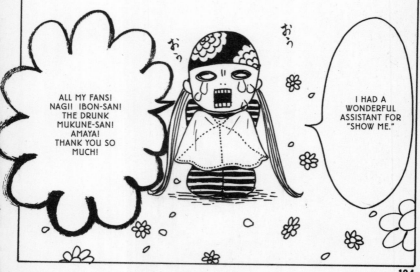

ALL MY FANS!
NAGI! IBON-SAN!
THE DRUNK
MUKUNE-SAN!
AMAYA!
THANK YOU SO
MUCH!

I HAD A
WONDERFUL
ASSISTANT FOR
"SHOW ME."